Judging God

It is Time to Judge Religions and Their Gods

by

John A. Henderson, MD

and

Craig Gurgew

2007

Parkway Publishers, Inc.

Boone, North Carolina

Books by John A. Henderson, MD

God.com: A Deity for the New Millennium

Fear Faith Fact Fantasy

Library of Congress Cataloging-in-Publication Data

Henderson, John A. (John Arthur), 1923-
Judging God / by John Henderson and Craig Gurgew.
p. cm.
Includes index.
ISBN 978-1-933251-42-4
1. Religious addiction. 2. Religion. 3. Religions. 4. Influence (Psychology)--Religious aspects. 5. Psychology, Religious. I. Gurgew, Craig. II. Title.
BL53.5.H46 2007
200--dc22
2007011749

Book and Cover Design by: Gina K. Cavallaro

DEDICATION

This book is dedicated to the millions of people who have suffered and are suffering at the hands of religions – all with the promise of eternal salvation and happiness *after* they die.

ACKNOWLEDGMENTS

We all stand on the shoulders of our predecessors and our colleagues. This is especially true when discussing the thousands of religions and gods.

We want to acknowledge some who have taken the time to criticize, correct, make suggestions, and support our efforts to be honest and logical in our discussion of a subject that is so divisive.

Herb Silverman, Victor Garrod, Ed Root, Joseph Cunningham, Michael Earl, Karon Park, Ed Buckner, Michael Goode, and Kirk Elwood have all made helpful suggestions.

A special thanks to William Harwood whose encyclopedic knowledge of religions and gods kept the authors from putting their foot in their mouth on several occasions.

The authors and only the authors are responsible for the thoughts and conclusions in this book. We are open to truth and would welcome a universal deity if one should decide to come forth.

Meanwhile, people should not remain silent when religions are used to the detriment of society.

TABLE OF CONTENTS

FOREWORD

As we began this book, we set out to disclose the harm caused by the world's religions. Our book was going to be a subdued, objective analysis of the historical oppression of philosophy, science, education, medicine, and morality by religions and its leaders. The content of our joint effort was to be a concise collection of data gathered over thousands of years by historians. We were going to keep our opinions out of the book and just state the facts.

But while doing the research for this book we realized that something was just not quite right. Our hearts did not seem to be one hundred percent into what we were writing. Chapter after chapter evolved as we methodically wrote material that was nothing more than a history lesson. Thousands of books have been published by historians and we did not consider ourselves historians.

Writers such as Carl Sagan and Bertrand Russell have written books objectively discussing religion. Thomas Paine's *Age of Reason,* Bertrand Russell's *Why I am Not a Christian,* and Dr. Henderson's previous books *God.com: A Deity for the New Millennium* and *Fear Faith Fact Fantasy* all discuss the illogical beliefs of a supernatural being. While informative, these works try to be non-confrontational and generally use care not to antagonize the church and its believers.

The church and its leaders influence government, the judicial system, the education system, and a large portion of the business community. Most nontheist writers find themselves in a dilemma. They do not want to step on the toes of the church because of fear – the same fear the church has used to control the masses for thousands of years.

We decided, however, that we *did* want to step on some toes. Why not? The church has been stomping on toes for thousands of years, and still does. Consequently, we decided to make our book more subjective; after all, religion is completely subjective. We decided to take off the gloves and call it the way we see it. No holds barred. Millions of good decent people feel exactly the same way. They live their lives in constant torment while pretending to believe in something that their brain tells them just is not so. These people are not just the uneducated – they are doctors, lawyers, engineers, pilots, educators, and politicians. Most people feel they must remain in the closet for a multitude of reasons. Social, professional, and family pressures force these otherwise intelligent human beings to go through life pretending that there is a supernatural being controlling their lives. Instead of trying to explain religion and god in scientific terms, we decided to boldly proclaim that god, at least one like the Jewish, Christian, Muslim (JCM) god, does not and cannot exist.

We are not scientists, nor are we researchers in biology, astronomy, or physics but we know as much about god as any theologian. We do not know where and when human life originated. We do not know where space ends or if it does. We do not know when or where life began or whether there are other intelligent civilizations in the universe. Nevertheless the secular people of the world are happier for accepting their ignorance, even though they remain curious and open-minded about the natural world. Secular people are full of hope that in due course our ignorance of the world and the universe will give way to a better knowledge and that we human beings will be empowered to deal with the problems of disease, environmental degradation, and other intractable issues. Devoutly religious people, on the other hand, must constantly worry that the growing knowledge of science will undermine their theologies and worst still, undermine their faith.

After interviewing professionals in mainstream America, we realized how many people are crying out for relief from religious doctrine and dogmatism. They are not afraid of an angry jealous god. They are not afraid of death. They *are* afraid of their bosses, their spouses, and their peers. They *are* terrified about losing their jobs, marriages, and friendships if they reveal their doubts about religion. They *are* afraid of people who commit dastardly crimes in the name of god and religion.

We are not theologians, but we know as much about god as Billy Graham, Jerry Falwell, and Pat Robertson. God has not talked to them and he has not talked to us either. (At least we are honest.) He has not talked to President George W. Bush, although the President might like to think otherwise. Mortals, not the divine father, correctly predicted what would happen after the invasion of Iraq.

If there is a supreme being, we do not know him/her/it. A supreme being, if one exists, has chosen to remain quiet while humans invent every kind of god imaginable. Man has created thousands of gods. Some of these men appointed themselves as the directors of communication between man and god – we of course have no evidence that these directors of communication are actually talking to their gods.

The sheer ridiculousness of religious superstition should keep people from believing it. The myths and stories that man has made up over the centuries are incredible. One would think that in the 21st century we would have long ago cast aside folklore to explain the uncertainties of life. While believing in the unbelievable is everyone's right, we take exception to the harm and damage these beliefs have caused and are causing. Millions have been murdered, executed, and imprisoned due to differences in religious beliefs. Scientific advances have been suppressed by the church. Even today, the church tries to dictate to science what it considers right and wrong. The world is full of anger, hate, and rage due to religious differences. Billions of dollars are needlessly spent on war because two religions, claiming to believe in the same god, cannot agree on small details of their doctrines. Millions of humans suffer needlessly from disease and hunger, and if not caused by a loving god, is certainly accepted and tolerated by it.

Since a person cannot be reasoned out of something he was never reasoned into in the first place, we decided to take a new approach. Although we realize that we may be shunned, excommunicated, and chased down by shotgun wielding Christians,

Jews, and Muslims, we still decided to proceed with this approach.

Hell hath no fury like a man whose god has been criticized. But we also know the time has come for man to judge the Jewish-Christian-Muslin (JCM) god. God must be judged on his actions and inactions. God must be judged by what he/she/it does, not by what someone thinks he said or did. We mortals think nothing of judging our peers, friends, parents, children, politicians, and criminals. However, the issue of judging god is off-limits to most. Our parents and clergy have brainwashed us into accepting the unconditional terms of god's doctrine. We are bombarded with fear tactics to prohibit us from remotely challenging this divine creature.

The time has come for all human beings to stand up to god and hold him accountable for all the rape, theft, torture, child abuse, and mass murder that he has not only condoned, but actually ordered over the centuries. In the same manner a serial killer is brought to justice in front of his peers, god should also be brought to justice. Thus we have titled our book *Judging God.*

You might ask, why not leave the believers to their religions? Why not leave the cultists to their cults? We would certainly agree to that, were there not so much hatred, anger, and harm done in the name of god and religion. We can paraphrase Thomas Jefferson and admit that whether an individual believes in one god, three gods, or thirty gods does harm to no one, but what one does in the name of religion or in the name of god is causing great harm in the world today.

We can only hope that truth and reason will prevail over myth and superstition, but that will only occur when scientists and reasoning people have the courage to speak out when people of faith spout out their intolerant, harmful views.

For generations religions have loudly criticized agnostics, nontheists, and atheists, even threatening them with an eternity of hell. Now that a few nonbelievers in the supernatural have acquired the courage to speak out against the myths, superstitions, and immoralities of religions, the religionists are screaming "foul play."

Lest readers get upset with the authors for judging and criticizing god, it should be noted that Abraham questioned god in the beginning (Genesis 18: 23-25).

If narrow-minded bigots are offended by this book, so be it!

CRITICAL ANALYSIS

On any given Sunday, the pastor of a church congregation totes his bible back and forth across the stage, reciting scriptures such as Psalm 105:1, "Thank the Lord for all the glorious things he does." All of the good, heaven-bound, god-fearing folks sit silently with stoic faces as their watches advance ever so slowly toward noon. Gosh, will twelve o'clock ever get here? Most do not even know what the pastor is saying. After all, the rules for heaven only require belief in Jesus, not listening to the preacher. However, one person sitting in the back row is listening intently to every word and attempting to follow the logic and the content of the sermon. Following the sermon, the listener patiently waits for the question and answer session that is sure to follow. But it never comes. What? No questions allowed? What about my opinion? Doesn't anyone want to hear my thoughts on the matter? Sadly the answer is no!

All humans, including the pious, critically analyze their everyday activities and transactions to verify the truthfulness of what they are told. A person cashing a check at the bank will not accept the cash until it is counted and verified. A couple buying a new home will not accept the realtor's claim of value until they have had an appraisal. A patient who is told he is terminally ill will consult another physician to verify the diagnosis. In essence, we verify to the best of our ability *all* claims to ensure their accuracy – except claims made by religion. Religious claims and dogma do not allow for a critical analysis of truthfulness. They must be blindly accepted as truth regardless of the ridiculousness of the claims. People spend their entire lives and fortunes worshiping an unverified god because a preacher says that a particular god exists. How strange it is that we will not accept a claim made by a highly educated, intelligent physician, but easily accept a claim made by an uneducated, unemployed wanderer like John the Baptist who lived in the woods and ate locusts and wild honey while wearing clothing made from camel hair.

Religion, by using fear, intimidation, and threats, does not allow for any dissension or differences of opinion. This attitude began fifteen hundred years ago during the Dark Ages and continued through the Inquisition all the way to the 21st century. During that time, the church successfully squelched science, art, and literature by gaining total control of the citizens' lives and minds. Dissenting viewpoints were not allowed and this stance continues today in modern religion. This is the way it is and if you have a critical opinion, you are going to hell. Period. End of discussion!

For mankind to advance in any human endeavor, critical analysis is necessary. As Socrates stated, "The unexamined life is not worth living." Most lectures in our society allow for open discussion, opinions, and even outright criticism. Scientists and medical researchers publish their work in scholarly publications and in trade journals and allow open discussions of their findings and ideas. They welcome outside input. For example, a researcher attempting to develop a vaccine for the bird flu holds open forums for his colleagues to give them the opportunity to challenge his results and offer different ideas on how to make the serum more effective with fewer side effects. Some may agree with his theory while others might disagree, but by using thoughtful and considered criticism as a tool, the researcher attempts to strengthen his research.

Freedom of speech allows critical analysis. Our politicians accept different viewpoints concerning the governing of our cities, states, and country. The President takes questions after a speech concerning federal policy. Many of these questions are contrary to the President's beliefs and may make him squirm at the podium. At least opposing viewpoints are publicly heard and tolerated. In many cases, the viewpoints and policies of an administration will actually change with public opinion and criticism. Sadly, our churches do not seem to believe in this type of freedom of expression and do not allow challenges to hierarchy, thereby maintaining total control of their congregations.

To openly challenge religious dogma in church would be ruinous to the clergy and their pocketbooks. As an eight-year-old, the co-author (CG) was actually dismissed from Sunday school due to asking questions that were not allowed. When the teacher was asked why god was so cruel and why he killed millions because of his jealousy, this eight-year-old boy found himself suddenly sitting on the sidewalk on a cold and blustery Sunday morning. Wrong question! "You may leave now, young man. I'm going to tell the rest of the children how good God is." As a consequence, it did not take long for this future author to figure out that Sunday school and Bible school were not for inquisitive minds – they were exclusively for those who allowed themselves to be brainwashed.

The author (JAH) was not kicked out of Sunday school, but years later his Sunday school teacher told him that he not only asked too many questions, but he was always there with his perfect attendance. She thought that at least he should have missed a few classes.

Facts concerning medicine and science can be proved to be either right or wrong. With enough facts and supporting data, a new treatment can be established. If the facts are not established, then something else can be tried. Listen to different opinions and criticism and move on. Do not be afraid to change your ideas and beliefs. There is nothing wrong with admitting failure, for failure is the pathway to future success. The church rarely admits failure of its doctrine. If it did, it would allow open criticism and challenge of its dogma. Carl Sagan in his *The Demon-Haunted World* held that, "Religious doctrine that is insulated from disproof has little reason to worry about the advance of science." Sagan realized that the church would accept truth only when it was obvious to the multitudes. The church would then simply maintain that it was the way god meant it to be and would continue to preach the unproven and the unverifiable.

Religion recognizes that supernatural habitats such as heaven and hell cannot be disproved by current scientific methods. So they continue teaching the unbelievable to those who are desperately seeking the great afterlife reward. And should you have a question, the ushers will be glad to show you to the door. Do not forget to drop a little change in the basket before you leave.

While religious leaders shy away from critical analysis of their beliefs, creeds, and dogmas, they insist that the theory of evolution be looked at critically. They approach the topic of evolution from two angles: (1) evolution is just a theory and not a proven fact and (2) it is only fair to allow competing theories such as creationism and intelligent design be discussed along with evolution. This stance, of course, is utter nonsense. First, creationism and intelligent design are warmed over stories of Genesis dressed in scientific garb. Second, proving evolution false does not prove that the current religious doctrines are true. Third, unlike religious doctrines, scientific theories such as evolution are based on observation, analysis, and verification; not on faith and dogma. It is a feather in the cap of scientists to be able to overthrow reigning theories based on their research. In contrast, religious dogmas are falsifiable because they are based only on faith.

Who can argue against critical analysis of any subject – scientific or otherwise? It is the only way for mankind to advance. Religious believers single out evolution for critical analysis because they know that the theory of evolution strikes at the very heart of the Bible and that the account of the creation in Genesis is just a myth. Scientists believe that critical analysis should be conducted on all issues – scientific, religious, and moral.

Everyone should develop their own ability to evaluate and analyze, but when they do, religions will be the first to prevent such critical analysis. That is what happened during the Dark Ages – the church stamped out all criticism of its dogma. Sad to say, it still does. People must learn that it is not necessary to respect religious stupidity. They must learn that illusions and delusions are not sacred.

Those who now want critical analysis of evolution should best beware. When children learn to think, evaluate, and question, they just might learn to evaluate and question religious superstitions. Critical analysis would end religion as it exists today.

GENESIS

Humans have pondered the origins of the universe since they first developed inquisitive thought. They have developed thousands of explanations for the origins of life on earth and the origin of the universe. These accounts and explanations varied widely from culture to culture. The existence of a supernatural divinity was a common theme in many religions. The divinity usually took the form of an invisible god in the heavens above controlling events on earth below.

The early Egyptian and Roman civilizations created multiple gods to explain the unknown. Native Americans utilized gods to comfort themselves and to explain their surroundings. It is interesting to note that both so-called primitive cultures and allegedly advanced societies believed in a very similar god.

While the polytheistic belief in multiple gods was still the mainstay of religions, around 1000 BCE there emerged a new concept of a single, all-knowing, all-powerful, paramount god. This monotheistic god, according to biblical accounts, was the creation of Abraham, although there is no evidence that Abraham actually existed. Abraham's father, like his neighbors, worshiped idols and multiple gods, as was common for this period. Abraham, however, formulated the notion of a unified divine authority and began paying homage to a single creator. Abraham's ideas ultimately became the basis for the Jewish, Christian, Muslim (JCM) religions.

The belief in a single god led to the Tanakh or Old Testament. The Old Testament begins with Genesis, which describes the creation of man and the universe. It is important that the reader understands the significance of this single chapter and how it has influenced the development of human thought and events.

According to Genesis, god created man and the universe in six days. He made earth the center of the universe. The sun, moon, planets, and stars were all created to revolve around the earth and to serve man's needs. God also created plants, herbs, animals, fish, and fowl. He created woman for man, and in most interpretations, made her inferior to man.

Judaism, Christianity, and Islam, the three Abrahamic religions shared the beliefs in Genesis. Although they all believed in the same god described in Genesis, the three religions varied greatly in their specific beliefs. This chapter will concentrate on Christian doctrine and its preservation of the story in Genesis.

Christianity was adopted by the mighty Roman Empire as its official religion in the 4th century CE, and became the most powerful religion in the Western World. The city of Constantinople (now Istanbul, Turkey) was the original hub of the Roman Catholic Church. Centuries later, Rome became the center for the church and has been ever since. Christianity under the guidance of the Catholic Church and the power of the Roman government spread rapidly throughout Europe and eventually was imposed on other cultures and nations by the invading Christian conquerors.

To maintain control of its vast empire, the Roman Catholic Church had to protect the validity of Genesis. Two topics in this founding chapter of the Bible had to remain intact in order to preserve the integrity of the Christian belief system. These were (1) that earth was the center of the universe, and (2) that man was created by a supernatural, single god. Any contradictory evidence that proved either of these premises false would result in a total collapse of the most powerful, wealthiest, and most influential religion in the world. The belief in Genesis had to be preserved, even at the cost of human lives.

As the Roman Catholic Church became more powerful, with the support of Emperor Constantine and succeeding Roman Emperors, it began an extensive campaign to control heretics, freethinkers, and non-believers. Thomas Paine wrote, "The age of ignorance commenced with the Christian system." For over a thousand years the church successfully controlled the thoughts and behavior of citizens. This period is now known as the Dark Ages. Any dissenters were quickly subdued and reprimanded. Science and scientific thought were suppressed with the fear of eternal punishment after death. People were taught and believed that the earth was flat and the center of the universe. The few who thought otherwise kept their opinions to themselves. During this period from the 5th century CE through the 15th century, the Roman Catholic Church ruled the western civilized world.

The Dark Ages were considered a period of scientific stagnation and social rot. Philosophers and scientific inquirers conducted their daily activities in a furtive manner. However, as Europe entered the

15th century, skeptics and heretics refused to remain silent. Observations and opinions that had previously been privately hidden were being made public. Art, literature, and science gained widespread popularity and this period became known as the Renaissance. This rebirth of culture and knowledge began in Italy and revived human creativity, which had been suppressed by the Church for centuries.

Among those emerging in this new era were men of science and astronomy. Some of the greatest names in scientific history appeared during this period. Copernicus, Bruno, and Galileo are just a few of the many who boldly conducted experiments and made observations about the world around them. Their observations conflicted with the long-standing Christian doctrine outlined in Genesis. Copernicus developed the heliocentric theory that placed the sun at the center of the solar system. This idea was in direct conflict with Genesis' version of the earth being the center of the universe. Due to the fear of insulting the Church, Copernicus remained "in the closet" for most of his life. He kept his theories under wrap until his later years. Bruno did not fare as well because he chose not to remain silent about his observations of the earth. He boldly proclaimed that the earth rotated on its axis and orbited the sun. This was a no-no for the Church and Bruno was burned alive at the stake. Galileo spent his later years under Church-imposed house arrest for making similar observations. We now know that these men were correct and that their efforts laid the foundation for modern science despite the Church's desperate efforts to preserve its ancient myths and doctrines.

To suppress heresy, the Church established the Inquisition in the 13th century. Nonbelievers and skeptics, as well as anyone else challenging Genesis, were imprisoned, tortured, and executed. The Inquisition was a purging of Christian dissenters throughout Europe. It was the most cruel and inhumane episode of religious intolerance ever known until the present day. Men of philosophy, astronomy, and science were targets of the Inquisitors, primarily because they were rapidly unraveling Genesis. A breakdown in Genesis would have generated a domino effect ending with the total collapse of Christianity, the most powerful and wealthiest religion in the world at that time.

Several hundred years after the Inquisition, Charles Darwin's theories challenged Genesis, unlike anyone before. Based on extensive observations, Darwin postulated that all life evolved from the same source and that all life is interconnected. Darwin suggested that man was not unique and that he developed along with apes. His elegant evolutionary theory of man's development dispensed with the need for the supernatural creation myth of the Bible and caused much turmoil within the Church. The developments in modern biology and the potential developments of cures for hitherto incurable diseases are testaments to Darwin's ideas.

Darwin's ideas, however, were anathema to those who believed that the Bible was inspired by god and that it was literally true. Therefore, fundamentalist Christians have been waging war against Darwin ever since the publication of the ground-breaking *The Origins of Species.* Later chapters in this book will deal with the objections raised by the fundamentalists to Darwin's theories.

Despite the persistent and vocal objections from true believers, Darwin's ideas gained ascendancy because scientists realized that his theories form the unifying principles of biology. The force of his ideas eventually led the late Pope John Paul II to openly endorse evolution. He proclaimed that the theory is more than just a hypothesis and that evolution is compatible with the Christian faith. The ultimate authority of the Roman Catholic Church, the Vicar of Christ, announced that he believes it has indeed taken the physical body of man millions of years to evolve. The Pope, however, re-interpreted the story of creation by saying that god created man's soul.

As we will further demonstrate in subsequent chapters, religions greatly impeded the development of science and knowledge. Ancient beliefs in the supernatural remain a powerful force and have caused much harm and damage to the same humans that god was supposed to love and protect. These harmful effects continue today.

CREATIONISM

Questions regarding the origins of the universe, life on earth, and the ultimate death of all living things have no absolute scientific answers at this time, although we have a much better understanding of these crucial questions than the people who lived even one hundred years ago. For thousands of years, in the absence of scientific knowledge, man has sought answers to these baffling questions by invoking gods.

In invoking the help of gods to explain the nature of the universe we live in, first, man had to create gods. Humans have created their gods with their limited experience and knowledge. Since gods cannot be seen, felt, smelled, heard, or tasted, they have been created in the minds of the only species of animals that have cognitive abilities – man. Certainly the gods of the rest of the animal kingdom would be nothing like the gods created by man. Can you imagine a god created by a rat or a lion? Xenophanes could. He wrote in the sixth century BCE, "Ethiopians imagined their gods as black and snub-nosed, while Thracians imagined their god as blue-eyed and red-haired. But if horses or lions had hands and could draw and fashion works as men do, horses would draw gods shaped like horses and lions like lions, making the gods resemble themselves."

Once a god has been created, it becomes easy to shift the burden of unanswerable questions to it. This divine figure can now become the creator who is responsible for the origin of the universe and everything within it. Most religions, past and present, have used the Great Spirit in the Sky as the basis for their version of creation. Some used one god while others required many gods to get the earth up and running. Humans have been created in every imaginable way possible – from waving a magic wand to rolling clay in god's hands. In some instances, man was made for woman and in others, woman was made for man. Most gods threw in a little sin and evil to make the story more interesting. One can suppose that when men and women get together, a little sin and evil will occur. If god created angels, one must ask why he bothered with man?

Creation myths, just like gods, were developed long before the beginnings of Judaism, Christianity, and Islam. The Genesis story is just one of the thousands of myths that have been told to explain the origin of man and the universe.

We would like to emphasize the importance of understanding the role of creation myths throughout the history of civilization. There have been literally thousands of tales and beliefs that have attempted to explain the origins of man. These myths have been the glue to hold societies together; they have been the basis of identity for communities, tribes, and nations. Some American Indian tribes believed man walked out from the center of the earth to begin life on the surface; others believed man emerged from the depths of the oceans to start life; yet others believed man was chiseled out of stone. One must prudently ask if these are less believable than believing that a woman was created out of a man's rib. The JCM religions have numerous versions of creation, the best known being the creation of Adam and Eve as described in Genesis.

The creation myths were accepted on the basis of faith. But these creation myths eventually ran into Darwin's theory of evolution. Darwin postulated that all the life on earth has a common ancestor and all the life forms we see on earth today evolved from that common ancestor. According to Darwin, humans too descended from other animals and are genetically related to mammals including apes. This evolution, according to Darwin, took place over millions of years.

Darwin's ideas are in stark contrast to the supernatural tale told in Genesis where god created the world, animals, and Adam and Eve in six days. Extrapolating from the story of Genesis, theologians concluded that the world is 6,000 years old. While Genesis implies that the world was created for the benefit of man, Darwin says that man is the result of a long line of evolution and is not the pinnacle of creation. Man is one of the animals and is subjected to the same natural forces of evolution.

The myths of creation came into existence thousands of years ago before scientific understanding of astronomy, cosmology, biology, physics, and chemistry developed. Consequently, these myths depend on supernatural explanations. In contrast, the theory of evolution does not depend on one or more creators. According to Darwin, life developed through natural physical, chemical, and biological processes. Evolution provides an elegant explanation for the unity and diversity of life on earth. It is consistent with the geological understanding that the earth is five billion years old and it is consistent with fossil records. Evolution is being observed in our daily lives – observe bacteria developing immunity to over-used medicines.

Creationism and Intelligent Design (ID) are the result of reaction from the fundamentalist Christians who believe in the literal truth of the Bible. They were developed to counter the separation of church and state doctrine in American life and to counter the Supreme Court decisions against teaching of creation myths in science classes. The myth of creation and ID as told in Genesis is the back doorway of introducing the Bible into science classes.

Creationists have a problem accepting the idea that humans evolved from other species of animals such as monkeys and apes. To them it is despicable.

> How dare an evolutionist to claim that a wealthy, upscale socialite evolved from a tick-infested, ass-scratching chimpanzee! Surely, Darwin was on drugs! I can't believe that Darwin fellow has the audacity to say that I came from a stinking monkey. That's absurd! Monkeys don't own mansions, BMWs, or expensive jewelry. They don't even use the proper fork to eat their salads. And their golf game proves they are not like humans. Besides, everyone knows how I came to be. I came from the dust and the dirt in the ground! The Bible says so.

Although the concept of evolution leaves many unanswered questions, scientists are continually working to piece together the great mystery of the origin of life and the origin of the universe. Scientists explore any and all facts they observe, even if it requires a change in their thinking. This openness to change is totally contrary to that of the church. With advancements in DNA analysis, scientists now know that genetically, humans and bonobos are 99% alike. That is not superstition; that is not myth; that is nothing but undisputed, scientific data. Even before DNA analysis, surgeons recognized that many internal organs of humans and apes were identical in nature. This does not prove evolution, but it is a strong argument for some type of progressive evolutionary process. Rest assured, scientists will continue to explore all scenarios until eventually we have more than just superstition on which to base the creation of the universe.

The one common problem with all the creation myths is that none of them ever tell who or what created the creator. Who made the big guy? The Bible tells us that god existed forever. No one had to create it. However, if god existed forever without a creator, logic tells us that the universe could have existed forever without a creator. The same logic tells us that if a creator exists, a super creator must have preceded it and so on and so on. Most JCM believers will ignore the subject of who created their god, or just say it has always existed, or that it created itself. That is like saying your new Buick created itself. Hello? In actuality, faithful believers do not want to think about evolution since it defies all that they were brainwashed into believing as youngsters. These same believers also do not want to think about all of the other gods that have existed over the thousands of years. To explain one mystery with another mystery is fruitless. It is just as easy to believe that the universe has existed forever as it is to believe that a supernatural being has existed forever.

In one sense pantheism, or the belief that god is everything, is more logical than a god that is separate from all that it has created. In that scenario we are all part of that creator, from the simplest plants to the most complicated animal – man. If god has created everything, then everything should be deemed sacred including the lowly cockroach. All life on earth would function in harmony if everything were sacred.

The inability to grasp the totality of god, just as the five blind men could not grasp the totality of the elephant, should humble all of us with our limited ability to comprehend god. In that sense, Buddha was correct when he advised his followers not to waste time trying to describe or understand god, as god is indescribable and unknowable. Thus we should not waste our time talking, writing, or even thinking about god. We should all be patient and wait for the researchers and the scientists to discover the origin and the purpose of the universe. The scientists have already made great strides in understanding the origin of the universe. If total knowledge is a thousand miles long, our current knowledge is but an inch.

The authors of this book would be happy to follow Buddha's advice and not waste time trying to understand god if it were not for all of the intolerance, bigotry, and killing that was and is going on in the world today in the name of god.

PHILOSOPHY

Philosophy, or the love of wisdom, was the father of science and scientific thought. The early philosophers did not claim to have wisdom but more accurately, they sought wisdom. They sought truth. The desire for truth caused the philosophers to question all that they had been taught. They questioned whether the commonly accepted knowledge of the universe was true or just fabrications created by humans to explain the unknown. Understanding the real nature of the universe and the morality of man were the major topics in this quest for wisdom.

The Greeks were the most influential of the early philosophers in the Western Hemisphere. The significance of Greek philosophy is that for the first time in written history humans began challenging dogmatic assertions. The Greeks believed that multiple gods controlled the universe and created incredible myths around them. An entire culture believed that golden chariots raced across the sky and that the sun and the moon were the eyes of god. Modern people now laugh at those early myths. How could anyone believe anything so outlandish? But the Greeks were not stupid. Although they were highly intelligent, but like religious believers today, the Greeks were afraid of the unknown. Therefore, they created and believed the myths that attempted to explain the unknown world.

Early philosophers were not about to be deceived. Although they did not have modern scientific equipment to prove their theories, they did possess an uncanny ability to see beyond superstitions, fables, and myths. Philosophers promoted freethinking, or critical thinking among men, thus opening the door to modern science. Superstitions cannot coexist with prudent, logical reasoning. Reasoning by demonstration and verification became a unifying factor for all philosophers and scientists. Unfortunately, theological leaders have kept logic and reason under lock and key and this practice continues today. Philosophers have always been seen by religious leaders as the cause of controversy. They were, and still are, looked upon as troublemakers. Unlike scientists and physicians, philosophers had nothing to contribute to society except ideas. They did not discover the atom, nor could they remove a tumor, but had it not been for the bold assertions of philosophers we would still be living in the Dark Ages.

Socrates (469-399 BCE) was one of the most influential thinkers of the fifth century. This early philosopher strived for intellectual independence, and his willingness to call everything into question makes him the first advocate of critical thinking. Rather than abandon his commitment to philosophical inquiry, Socrates chose to face execution. The charge was undermining state religion "by not believing in the gods the polis believes in." We see these same charges 2500 years later!

Another influential freethinker was Epicurus, who was born half a century after Socrates' death. This radical thinker questioned the concept of gods and decided that if they do exist, they are not interested in mankind. He believed in equal rights for women and slaves, a subject that Christians refused to discuss for two thousand years. His *Epicurean Paradox* is the most logical, prudent argument for the nonexistence of a god that has ever been written. Philosophers and nontheists worldwide have used this writing as a cornerstone for their lack of belief in the supernatural:

> Is god willing to prcvent evil, but not able? Then he is not omnipotent. Is he able, but not willing? Then he is malevolent. Is he both able and willing? Then whence cometh evil? Is he neither able nor willing? Then why call him God?

Friedrich Nietzsche, the German philosopher, was famous, or infamous if you prefer, for claiming that god was dead. Nietzsche knew that god did not exist but he realized that the public would have difficulty accepting that fact. Even today the name Nietzsche causes a shiver and a sharp reaction whenever it is raised in the presence of god-believers.

Soren Kierkegaard, the Danish philosopher and theologian, was the bipolar son of a bipolar Christian minister. He concluded that god exists because people believed that god exists. Kierkegaard maintained, just as Martin Luther did, that one must accept Christianity based on faith alone. He is given credit for the word *fideism,* which translates into the belief that truth is based on faith. Simply put, his premise was that if you believed in something, that belief made it true. It should be obvious that the concept of fideism is patently untrue. As Nietzsche noted, "A casual stroll through a lunatic asylum shows that faith does not prove anything."

Blaise Pascal, the French scientist and philosopher noted for his wager, was so afraid of his god that he postulated the concept that it is better to believe in a god that does not exist rather than taking a chance on not believing in a god that does exists. He, like many believers was afraid that there just might be a cruel god waiting to zap him for an eternity if he did not worship it. Why take the chance? His argument is known as Pascal's wager.

On the other hand, there have been many philosophers such as Rene Descartes, Francis Bacon, and Bertrand Russell who have insisted that all truths, religious and scientific, must be subjected to reason, logic, and verification. The authors of this book fall into that group as they believe that logic and reasoning prove that god, at least a god like the Judeo-Christian-Muslim (JCM) god, does not exist except in the minds of people who believe that it does.

Unfortunately, some of our greatest thinkers, the philosophers of the world, will not offer much help in eradicating the harm of religion to mankind. Although most of these highly intelligent individuals realize that religion is nothing more than human fantasy, they must make a living like everyone else. There are not many jobs available for someone who does nothing but think. Just try to interview for a job when you are asked, "What is your greatest strength?" Your answer would be, "Well, I sit around the house or office and think." End of interview. Most philosophers have no choice but to seek employment at colleges and universities as teachers and instructors. Many of these institutions are funded by religionists who do not tolerate religious dissension. Consequently, rational freethinking intellects are forced to keep their mouths shut in order to keep their jobs. A question presented by the early Greek philosopher, Thales, was, "...what is wisdom good for if it can't pay the rent?"

On the other hand, conventional wisdom maintains that universities are filled with crazy liberals and that tenure protects them. Even so, the objective evaluation of the prevalent religion in society remains unaccomplished.

SCIENCE

Nothing has been more controversial in the history of the civilized world than the relationship between religion and science. For many ancient cultures this was not a problem since primitive civilizations had not discovered the concept of analyzing by scientific inquiry and there was only experience with trial and error. Many cultures such as the Babylonians and Aztecs had advancements in mathematics, calendar dates, and astronomy. These discoveries did not cause conflicts with their religious beliefs and were looked upon as contributions to the betterment of society. The existence of the local gods was not challenged.

Conflict began when man started replacing divine superstition with practical, inquisitive thought. The Greek philosopher Socrates was one of the most notable challengers to religious dogma. Socrates believed that knowledge could be gained by insistent questioning rather than by accepting blind, superstitious myths. During this era in Greek history many discoveries were made that began revealing the true nature of the earth and its inhabitants. Observations clearly demonstrated that the earth was round, not flat as most people believed at that time. These scientific discoveries were suppressed by religions since they contradicted their supernatural claims and dogmas.

Christianity thrust civilization into the Dark Ages. This religiously dominated era lasted for hundreds of years and was a period of social decline and scientific stagnation. Never before in written human history had religion maintained such a nefarious stance against inquisitive thought, scientific advancement, art, and literature. We will never know the full impact that this period had on modern civilization. We can only speculate what our world would be like if science and knowledge had not been stifled. Unfortunately, we still see religion's strong influence at work.

Many theologians and scholars claim that religion and science have and can work together in harmony. But if there has been a harmonious balance, this balance has only acted as a façade for the underlying conflicts that have always existed between the two. It is impossible for prudent, scientific thought to be compatible with pious folklore. The two will never mesh. Scientific claims are the result of logic, reason, intelligent observations, and verification. Contrarily, religious doctrine has never had any scientific basis and is only the unsubstantiated creation of the human mind, arising out of fear, ignorance, and hope. Religions accept science only when the results are obvious to all, and then maintain that their god intended it to be that way in the first place. Science can never win arguments that are not based on truth, reason, and proof. H.L. Mencken in *Treatise on the Gods* wrote, "The truth is that every priest who really understands the nature of his business is well aware that science is its natural and implacable enemy. He knows that every time the bounds of exact knowledge are widened, however modestly, the domain of theology is correspondingly narrowed."

In the world of science, it is accepted that you cannot prove a negative. Thus one cannot prove there is no god. Nevertheless, the godly folks with their religions and thousands of different sects allegedly prove that their god exists on faith alone. They cannot see, feel, hear, smell, or taste their god, but they are convinced that he exists. Based on human logic and reason, one *can* prove that no god, at least a god like the JCM god, could possibility exist.

There is a unique difference between science and religion – the right to question. Scientists thrive on allowing open debate and argument concerning their studies and theories. They welcome criticism from others in order to prove or disprove their claims. Trade journals, conventions, and think tanks are just a few of the tools used by scientific researchers to validate their opinions and experiments. A dissenting view of a fellow scientist is actually looked upon as a positive factor. Anger, revenge, and punishment of others who disagree or challenge have no place in the scientific world. Most scientific advancements have occurred due to the accumulation of many different ideas that eventually merged into one. Scientists realize that they add their bit of knowledge on the shoulders of their predecessors.

Reason is the mainstay of truth. Without reason and logic, there is no truth. Martin Luther maintained, "Reason is the devil's bride and God's worst enemy." Religious doctrine does not allow dissenting viewpoints or challenges. Religious leaders insist on total blind faith in accepting their claims, regardless of how ridiculous these claims may be. Authoritative religions such as Christianity and Islam have zero tolerance for those who object to their beliefs, while a few religions like Buddhism can maintain a peaceful coexistence with reason and logic.

To force intelligent human beings into believing the unbelievable requires authoritative religions to maintain a tight rein over its followers. Fear and intimidation are the methods for maintaining this control. Christians preach a torturous afterlife of eternal suffering for not believing their dogma. As history has repeatedly shown, this afterlife has been hastened for millions of challengers by torture and execution.

There is no question that many scientific facts about the earth are totally in conflict with religious claims. For example, we now know that the earth is round and is not the center of the universe. We also know that the earth has existed for billions of years, not 6,000 years. There is a good possibility that there are planets that are similar to earth and that some of those planets may support life as well. If that can be established by science, it will take away the uniqueness of earth in the cosmological scheme of things. Of course, it won't stop religionists from saying "That is the way God made the universe."

Technological advances in radiometric dating methods and DNA research have shown that there is a lineage between man and ape and that man's existence is due to a long drawn out process of evolutionary change and adaptation. As we enter into the twenty-first century we are finding ourselves on the scientific and medical threshold of cloning human beings. Although a very controversial issue with religious doctrine, cloning will ultimately prove that a human can be created without divine assistance. Scientists have already successfully cloned animals – Dolly was the first cloned mammal. Combined with advances in stem cell research, humans will soon have the ability to create organs and tissue to replace those damaged by disease or injury. Since praying to the intelligent designer has not had any effect on human progress or the elimination of suffering, our bold medical researchers are taking that burden upon themselves.

Although scientific knowledge has greatly diminished the prospect that there is, or ever was a divine creator, religion still dominates man's beliefs. When a scientist or a naturalist tries to turn on the light of truth, he is silenced in every possible way. That is the reason many scientists, most of whom do not believe in a supernatural being, refuse to debate the issue. Studies have shown that 96% of true scientists do not believe in a god like the JCM god with a devil, heaven, hell, and eternal life. However, most will not admit that publicly as they do not want to spend their time and effort trying to convince someone who cannot be convinced, no matter the facts. Most scientists are interested in understanding what is unknown, and openly share their information with other scientists. Trying to convince people who believe in faith and revelations is not worth the effort. Many scientists refuse to discuss or debate religion with people with strong faith because they know the religionists cannot be reached through reason.

Science and technology are separate fields but are closely related and intertwined. Science is systematic knowledge derived from observation and study. Technology is the practical application of science. While scientists are concerned with expanding the knowledge of the universe, technologists take their discoveries and convert them into inventions that benefit man. All of our wonderful gadgetry today, such as cell phones, computers, and satellites, originated from the laborious and often unrecognized work of scientists, many of whom have remained in a religious closet simply to prevent persecution. In an ironic twist, most religious organizations eagerly use this technology to enhance the preaching of superstitions and myths while ostracizing the very folks who made such technology possible. While attending a modern church service, one can only sit in awe and observe the surrounding technology, electronic lighting, musical equipment, climatic controls, and sound effects that make the preacher's booming voice more threatening to nonbelievers. Their computers record the donations that pay the preacher's salary. It rarely occurs to the clergy or to the congregation that many of the amenities that make their lives more enjoyable and comfortable originated from people not believing in god – the same people who are on a journey to hell and eternal damnation according to their beliefs.

Science and the technology that follows have dramatically improved the care of the ill and the suffering. No longer do we have to rely on charlatans and gods to heal the sick. Men and women of science and medicine, most of whom do not believe in the supernatural, have made marvelous advances in understanding and ultimately curing diseases, afflictions, and injuries. Amazingly, a devoutly religious person, after praying to god for a cure and getting no response, will zealously seek a doctor for healing. Then, after the doctor heals this devoutly religious person, he will return to church on Sunday and thank god for the miracle. God is once again number one, and the doctor is forgotten. We have come a long way from living in a cave around an open fire. It is science and technology that are responsible for these "miracles", with no thanks to religion.

As humans continue to place their lives and well being into the hands of a mythical divinity, progress in science will be a slow process. We will never know how much further ahead we would be today if we had not gone through the Dark Ages of religious control. To think that the Greeks had proven information on the earth and the universe that was subsequently squelched by religious organizations and replaced by superstitious, unbelievable dogma is astonishing. Science has been kept under wraps for centuries, and we still see religious leaders trying to control the minds of intelligent men and women who dare step outside the box and attempt to make our lives better and fuller.

Unfortunately, like so many of our earlier scientists, people choose to remain in the closet and conceal their true beliefs to avoid persecution and criticism. It is hoped that in the future, as our world becomes one, religious barriers will crumble and allow science and research to flourish.

A recent case is an example of religion interfering with science when science proves religion's myths false. Kenya national museum has on display fossils of hominids that show humans' early ancestors. This collection is one of the most important fossil findings in existence. The Evangelical Christian Church in Kenya is attempting to suppress the exhibit as it does not coincide with its dogma. Paleontologist Richard Leakey is contesting the removal of the exhibit and hopefully the publicity will keep this uniquc exhibit available to all who want to study it. The public must become aware and speak out against the efforts of religion to squelch all scientific studies that do not reinforce church dogmas, superstitions, revelations, and ancient myths.

We must acknowledge that due to science we have reached a point where humans have the capability of destroying most, if not all of life on earth. The products of science that make our lives more comfortable and enjoyable are also capable of destroying us. The nuclear energy we use for electricity is also used in the atomic bomb. The rockets that we use to explore distant planets are the same rockets we use to deliver these bombs. The laser beam we use to perform surgery is the same laser beam we use to guide the rocket carrying the bombs. As we enter into the twenty-first century, we must insure that our scientific advancements are only used to better mankind. Extreme religious fanatics are actively pursuing access to nuclear weaponry to further their cause. The probability is high that the next nuclear bomb to explode will be the result of minute differences between the beliefs of the people claiming to worship the same god. And some people are just "religious" enough to do it.

We need to remind ourselves that most of the good things in our lives today, from automobiles to televisions, are products of science and technology with no help from god.

SCIENCE VS RELIGION

Following the death of Jesus, apostles such as Paul, the apostle to the gentiles, spread Christianity across the Middle East. Along with Paul's efforts came the gospels and other propaganda material.

Long before Jesus was born, Greeks were developing philosophy, mathematics, and attempting to explain the natural world. The Greeks were the first people to try to explain the natural world without the aid of gods and other supernatural beings.

At the time of Jesus' birth, science and theology were both in their infancy. At that time Christians were beginning to formulate Christian theology while no one had yet developed the concept of science and the scientific method. By the time Christianity took hold, the knowledge that was developed by the Greeks had been forgotten. The Bible, said to be the word of god, dominated European thought.

Two thousand years after the birth of Jesus, Christian theology is still steeped in supernatural concepts and explanations such as the virgin birth, resurrection, trinity, the holy ghost, life after death, heaven, and hell. According to this theology the faithful will be absolved of all sin and sent to heaven while the wicked will be sent to hell.

At the end of the Dark Ages, science started taking shape. Initially, science also was steeped in astrology and attempts to convert base metals into gold. The scientists at that time did not have any better idea of the natural world than did theologians.

Now at the beginning of the twenty-first century, theology remains substantially the same but science and its offspring technology have made great advancements.

Astronomers now know, unlike the writers of the Bible, that the earth is not the center of the universe. Earth is but a trivial planet among billions of galaxies, stars, and solar systems. The universe is much more complex than was ever imagined by primitive man or the gospel writers. They had no idea of the vastness of the universe and they had no idea that the sun did not rotate around the earth. Many religionists still believe the earth is only 6,000 years old but most people, irrespective of their religious persuasion, accept the fact that the earth revolves around the sun.

Physicists now have a better understanding of how the universe operates: how the universe began; how the elements were formed from the primordial fireball after the big bang; how the galaxies and stars formed when the universe came into existence; how vast the universe is in terms of distances.

Physicists discovered that the ultimate building blocks of matter unlocked vast energy in the form of nuclear power – which can be used for both good and evil purposes. They were stunned to realize that some of the rules that apply to the world do not always apply to protons, electrons, and other building blocks of matter.

Chemists did not truly understand the concepts of the elements, molecules, and atoms until the 19th century. Our modern world immensely benefited from the advances made by the chemists – in terms of comfort, agriculture, and medicine.

Medicine is no longer dependent on gods, prayers, and superstitious myths. Physicians and medical researchers have vast knowledge of how the body works, how chemicals interact within our bodies, the causes of diseases, how to conquer diseases that used to kill millions of people, and how to anticipate the development of epidemics.

People with mental diseases were thought to be possessed by the devil and most religions developed rituals to treat those diseases. Failing to cure them, the patients were left to fend for themselves or die. Psychologists and psychiatrists now have a much better handle on psychiatric diseases. Neuroscience is probing deeper and deeper into the workings of the brain and unlocking its secrets.

Biologists showed that man is not a unique creature, i.e., a special creation of an all-powerful, all-knowing god. We now know that we share our genes with primitive life forms and that we share our origins with them. It took millions of years to evolve from lifeless chemical soup to self-replicating chemicals to one-celled life forms to bacteria to plants to animals to dinosaurs to apes and to man. Most of the life forms that evolved over millions of years became extinct and the earth is not going to miss humans if they become extinct. Humans are not superior to any other life forms on earth and are like everything else, subject to the natural forces that control the earth.

Geologists found that the earth was not static and was made up of tectonic plates and that the movement of these plates caused earthquakes. Most people today realize that earthquakes are not the result of god's anger toward us; they are the result of mindless movements of the plates. Most people also realize that tornadoes, hurricanes, blizzards, and all other weather phenomena are not the result of some god getting angry. They are the result of the atmosphere that surrounds us, the way the earth tilts towards the sun, and the earth's revolving around the sun. Again, no mysterious and unpredictable god at work.

Look at the technology we now have at our disposal. Even Roman emperors did not have access to such power and conveniences. Who needs chariots when we have a Rolls Royce? We can take a dip in the Atlantic Ocean in the morning and put our toes in the Pacific Ocean in the afternoon. We can pick up a phone and talk to someone on the other side of the globe. We can watch live when the President of the United States speaks at a press conference.

If the gospel writers came to life and walked on the streets of New York City today, they would think that they were in heaven. Those writers could not have imagined in their wildest dreams what we now have. On the other hand, they would have no difficulty understanding present day theology – it hasn't changed much.

The dramatic advances in our knowledge will continue, barring some earth shattering events such as nuclear war or a global calamity. Scientists will continue to unlock the secrets of nature and will continue to make the lives of human beings more comfortable.

None of these worthwhile advances would have been accomplished had scientists stuck to the Bible!

Science and technology are increasing by leaps and bounds; religion remains stuck in two thousand year old superstition and myth. Although religionists would like to take credit for science, science and religion cannot co-exist. Science is based on truth and the verification of that truth; religion is based on ignorance, hope, superstition, and myth. As science increases, religion is diminished. When the universe is finally understood, god will disappear.

MEDICINE

The further we look back in history, the more closely we see medicine intertwined with religion and superstitious beliefs. Most cultures assumed that diseases and infections had divine origins and were the result of evil spirits and satanic gods. Priests and medicine men were often one and the same. They claimed to have direct connections with the heavenly gods and could cure disease and illness by performing colorful rituals such as walking on hot coals and sacrificing helpless animals. These actors were more like modern day televangelists than present day physicians.

Many religions considered the dead body sacred and forbade any sort of post mortem dissection, even to learn the causes of illness and death. Many thought that tampering with the physical body after death would interfere with their afterlife. This was the beginning of religion influencing and hindering the study of medicine and it continues today. Most religions have their own set of ethical laws pertaining to medicine, drugs, and medical research. They brainwash their believers into forgoing transfusions, transplants, and other treatments in order to reserve a divine seat in the hereafter.

Religion promises comfort as well as physical and spiritual health after death while medicine tries to provide these before death. One can only guess how many people have needlessly suffered their entire lives because of their religion, only to die and never learn that the pie in the sky does not exist as they are totally, irreversibly, permanently dead. Children as well as adults have suffered and died waiting for god to cure them. An article in the journal *Pediatrics,* April 1998, found in a study of 172 child deaths that when medical treatment was withheld on religious grounds, 140 of those children would have had at least a 90% likelihood of survival with medical care.

The deaths of children who were denied proper medical care because of their parents' religious beliefs are the most heart breaking because, by law, the parents' religious wishes override those of children. Children are denied their say in their own medical treatment.

Medicine, when compared to some of the other professions, is in an enviable position. Everyone can see that it has been man and science that has worked unceasingly to ease the pain and suffering of humanity. Many people believe that everything that happens is god's will. This would be true if there *were* an all-powerful, all-knowing, supernatural being. Few people refuse the benefit of medical science when they are suffering, but after benefiting from the efforts of medical science many will give credit to god instead of the medical profession. Presently god takes no blame or responsibility for disease or illness, but it does not mind getting credit for the cure. If god is the creator of everything, then it must be responsible for the smallpox virus, AIDS, and bubonic plague.

Physicians are in the forefront when it comes to witnessing the absurdities of human suffering. Day in and day out they are confronted with severe birth defects, debilitating diseases, and traumatic injuries.

Most people will never experience the dilemma of a six-year-old with brain cancer. They will never observe the burnt corpses from an airplane crash and most likely will never have to raise a child afflicted with cerebral palsy. These are things we see on the morning news and if they become too repulsive we change the channel. Most do not want to, or have to deal with it. Physicians deal with these human tragedies daily. Most physicians during the early stages of their education recognize the discrepancies between religion and medicine. It is practically impossible not to do so. What religion claims to be god's will takes on an entirely different meaning on the operating table. When the sole survivor of a terrible airplane crash is an eight-year-old boy who may experience severe pain and suffering the rest of his life, one must question god's mercy and judgment. While the religious folks are praising god for this miracle of life, they refuse to comment on the one hundred fifty others who died horrendous deaths. They are not the ones who have to examine the fried bodies and meet with the parents, spouses, and children and explain that their loved ones are nothing more than unrecognizable charred remains.

Men and women of medicine, including the researchers, have discovered many of the causes of mental and physical ailments. Medical diseases such as leprosy were once thought to be the work of the devil. Warts, tumors, and other noticeable body abnormalities were the trademarks of witches who were considered the messengers of Satan. Neurological disorders such as depression, neurosis, retardation, epilepsy, and multiple sclerosis were definitely proof of the devil at work. Witches and other not-so-perfect humans were imprisoned and executed to eliminate the devil from society. In nineteenth century America, thousands of mentally impaired people were confined in institutions for life, locked away and forgotten. Thankfully, medicine and science has finally exposed these conditions as being caused by chemical imbalances, congenital defects and so on, not the work of the devil.

Today modern doctors live in a world of ambiguity, attempting to balance religion and medical science while witnessing first hand the cruel, unexplainable medical conditions of their patients. They observe the devout Christian dying of a rare malignancy with no cure in sight while the family members gather around the bedside and pray to their loving god for a miracle. The miracle never happens and the poor patient who has worshiped this loving god his entire life dies in severe pain and torment. Now the doctor notices the family praising god, even as god refused to answer their prayers. They thank god for relieving their loved one of suffering and for taking the poor fellow to heaven. They claim it is a miracle and cannot wait to get to church and tell everyone what a wonderful god their Almighty is.

For a physician to remain a believer is all but impossible. Somewhere the intellect must kick in and override the religious and supernatural beliefs that he/she was taught as a child. The blinders must fall to allow the doctor to recognize and separate reality from superstition. As these realities set in, the modern physician must also realize the social, professional, political, and familial consequences of disclosing atheistic or agnostic beliefs. He would lose patients. His family would suffer from rejection and ridicule. Therefore, he remains in the Copernican closet and pretends to be a devout religious follower. He spends his life aware of a suffering humanity that is not relieved by an all-powerful, loving, intelligent creator.

Many "Christs" and medicine men throughout history were supposedly capable of healing the sick and raising the dead. There is no evidence to support any of these miracles. Even today charlatans make such claims. While physicians realize there are examples of medical "miracles", they also realize that these rare occurrences are not the result of divine intervention. Occasionally a disease will go into remission, even be cured for no known reason. These remissions and cures occur in atheists and nonbelievers as often as in devout believers. Why would an intelligent creator save a sinner from a deadly disease, only to send his soul to hell a few years later? Might as well go ahead and do it now and be done with it. Medical professionals question intelligent design and more often than not, see unintelligent design.

The advances in medicine have been slowed by the inane sadistic belief that god meant for men and women to suffer and die. When Benjamin Franklin discovered the lightning rod, some said it was immoral and interfered with god's plan to strike down sinners with bolts of lightning. When the discoverer of anesthesia used chloroform to relieve the pain of childbirth, a clamor arose that god meant for women to suffer in childbirth because Eve sinned in the Garden of Eden. Needless to say, that did not have much effect on women in pain from childbirth and it won't have much effect on coming generations of women, even if god does want all women to suffer in the future. We can be sure that continued progress in medicine will be made as man continues to prevent pain and suffering and attempts to defer our ascent into heaven.

Religions' interference in medical advancements continues to this day, especially concerning sexual activities, the so-called below the belt issues. Fundamentalists continue to spout their inane stupidities that AIDS is god's punishment to homosexuals, never explaining why god does not limit that dreaded disease to the homosexuals. How can anyone believe in a god that gives AIDS to innocent women and children? Throughout history god has spread its punishment of sinners to those who were innocent, even on to their future generations.

Religions continue to prevent advancement in the field of genetics under the belief that god creates life and does not want man to tinker with it. The concept that god wants nothing to interfere when a one cell live sperm unites with a one cell live ovum is as silly and illogical as the premise that god created smallpox and does not want man fooling with it.

Fortunately, man will continue to do research and continue to search for the relief of pain and suffering in spite of the teaching that life is sacred and not to be touched by man. All can see who will look, what a poor job god is doing with congenital defects and other medical disasters. Only the most fearful and misguided will not support studies to improve life for the human race.

Unfortunately, religious beliefs will slow and perhaps even prevent some medical research. The political power of religion is strong enough to cause politicians to enact laws to prevent medical research and the use of that research, which would alleviate human suffering. Thus, we see laws preventing the day-after pill and laws preventing women from choosing the medical care they desire. In the not-so-distant past, *all* contraceptives were illegal, thanks to certain religious groups and their influence over politicians.

It is not within the realm of this book to speculate why males – no females allowed – created their gods and religions with so many sexual hang-ups and why they continue to this day. William Harwood in his book, *Priestly Power and the Role of Sin in a Humanist in the Bible Belt,* maintains that as long as sin was defined as the unnecessary hurting of a fellow sectarian, the masses did not sin for years. Persons who did not sin did not need to buy salvation from a priest. It was therefore in the interest of the priestly caste to invent sins so that the masses would commit them. The way to do that was to impose severe and absurd restrictions on who could engage in sexual recreation and where, how, and with whom. All but the most chronic masochists would refuse to comply. Thus, lust, masturbation, even heavy petting became a sin.

While we can see how religions are interfering with medical advancements, we should not get too depressed as in the end, society will do what is best and most comfortable for man. More and more folks will come to realize that society must find the solutions to human problems because if there is a god, it must surely be resting and is not paying much attention to its subjects. Perhaps the Deists are correct when they maintain that after god created man and the universe, he went into retirement.

When people are made to believe that god will protect them and cure them if only they have enough faith, the benefits of modern medicine are neglected. Fortunately, that belief affects only the individual involved and his immediate family, not society in general. Recently an autistic child was smothered to death as religious zealots attempted to drive Satan out of her body. Many Christian Scientists refuse medical care because they believe god will take care of them. However, most backslide when faced with pain and suffering, although many continue to believe that god will cure them in spite of evidence to the contrary.

Religions will continue to interfere with the advancements of medicine under the guise of preventing man from taking over god's responsibility, but in the meantime physicians must continue to "play god" until god decides to "play doctor."

MORALITY AND SIN

In this chapter we will deal with the concepts of morality and sin and how those ideas are central to the control exerted by organized religions.

Morality is a code of behavior – a set of guiding principles for humans for treating each other. Sin, on the other hand, is a transgression against god.

The JCM religions claim that god gave humanity the Ten Commandments – our moral code. Religionists claim that without god telling us what is right and what is wrong, mankind will sink into amoral behavior and that without god's commandments we would behave like all other animals.

God's Ten Commandments are: do not have any other god but me; do not make images of me; keep the Sabbath; do not use my name in vain; honor your parents; do not commit murder; do not commit adultery; do not steal; do not bear false witness against your neighbor; do not covet your neighbor's house, wife, slave, ox, donkey, or anything that belongs to him. In reality, however, the Bible lists over 600 commandments in addition to these ten.

Morality did not originate with the ten commandments. Morality is older than religion. All societies have moral codes. The first individuals on earth who came together as a family, clan, tribe or society established codes of behavior in order to live in harmony with one another. Morality helped them to survive as individuals and as a group. Such a code of behavior is the basis of human morality.

Morality is a sense of what is right or wrong. We have no difficulty in understanding the purpose of the Ten Commandments – respecting neighbors' property rights, the need for controlling sexual urges in order to live in harmony with others in the society, the dangers of engaging in aggressive acts towards others, and treating one's parents and elders with respect. Whether you believe in god or not, these concepts make sense.

However, morality does not remain static. While on the broader level, major concepts do not change, specifics do change. Human morality will continue to evolve as societies evolve. Communication among nations and societies has improved so much that people modify their notions of morality. For example, god in his commandments talks about male and female slaves but never says that it is wrong to have slaves. We now recognize that it is utterly unacceptable to own slaves. We extend the concept to child labor – we prohibit child labor and encourage all nations to adequately care for children by providing them food, shelter, and education. In that sense we have improved upon god's commandments.

The world's increasing population, global commerce, advancing knowledge, science, and the demands for equality require ever changing and evolving moralities. The earth and its environment are rapidly changing with the increasing population and the pollution caused by people, industries, and automobiles. The simple concept of "the solution to pollution is dilution" is no longer valid, as pollution is accumulating faster than the earth can absorb it. These changing conditions require still more refined moral behavior. For example, at the time of god's commandments we did not know that tobacco was responsible for cancer of the lung. Once we understood that, we took steps to control its consumption. In doing so, we had to trample on the rights of tobacco farmers as well as smokers. Even though god was silent on the use of tobacco (god did not know about the harmful effects of tobacco when he was dictating the Bible), we now understand the consequences of its use and have started moving toward our own commandment, "Thou shalt not smoke tobacco." That is moral evolution. Also, it is no longer valid, nor is it moral, to believe that god wants babies to be conceived whenever there is sex.

The morality of biblical times has little in common with that of today except for the universal beliefs that man should not cheat, steal, or kill, and should follow the golden rule of treating others the way you would like to be treated. These universal admonitions predate churches, gods, and religions. They are universal humanistic concepts and are an integral part of our code of conduct. They allow people to live together in harmony. Morality is a product of human development and not a product of a supernatural being's need to tell us what is right or wrong.

Sin, on the other hand, originated with the advent of religion. Sins were transgressions against god's desires as interpreted by the clergy. They differed with each belief system and each god. Sins were created in the minds of men, and then projected to their gods – then back to man. It was the clergy's way to control their followers' beliefs and actions.

When Christianity became the established religion of the Roman Empire and the church wanted to persuade followers of other savior gods such as the sun god Mithra to switch to Jesus, it simply absorbed such Mithraic beliefs as December 25th for the god's birthday and Sunday as the god's sacred day of rest and worship, rather than Saturday, which was the seventh day of the week. To attract worshipers of the Germanic sex goddess, Frig, who ate the vulva-shaped fish that was her sacramental body on her name day, Frigday, the Pope made Friday fish day in Christianity and maintained that this was god's desire. It has also been said that the Pope wanted to support fishermen, so he required all of his followers to eat fish on Friday and maintained that this was god's desire. It became a sin not to follow god's rule to eat fish on Friday. Amazingly, many Catholics still eat fish on Friday. Were it not for those religious instructions, December 25th would be a time of winter festival and Sunday would be no more holy than any other day. Sins are frequently translated into human immorality when the church has the power to make that happen.

Just as the concept of morality has changed over time, so too has the concept of sin changed over the last two thousand years. The results of a recent United Kingdom poll shows that its respondents believed that a new set of sins should replace the seven Deadly Sins devised by Pope Gregory the Great during the sixth century. The original sins identified by Pope Gregory were anger, gluttony, sloth, envy, pride, lust, and greed. The new sins according to the poll should be cruelty, adultery, bigotry, dishonesty, hypocrisy, selfishness, and greed. Only greed has survived the centuries as a sin.

As the world changes, our attitudes towards right and wrong also change. Not many people seem to be worried about cooking a young goat in its mother's milk or keeping the meat of the Passover lamb overnight. Those issues were serious sins just two thousand years ago.

It is not considered a sin for animals – except human ones – to kill, lust, copulate, covet, fight over food, or defecate in the woods nor do we consider it immoral, as lower animals do not have souls to be judged. Only man commits sin. Only man strives to control human behavior by using people's fear of a supernatural being. Once the clergy have convinced people that god does not like homosexuality, multiple sexual partners, or women preachers, those activities become an issue for human morality and human ethics. Those desires of god become firmly established and along with the concept of a perfect unchanging god, become etched in stone and become part of common law.

God did not make slavery immoral and illegal; man did. God did not make inequality of women immoral; man did. God did not make polygamy immoral and illegal; man did. God did not make environmental pollution immoral and illegal; man did. God did not make tribal wars, civil wars, and world wars a sin. If war is ever to be made immoral and illegal, it will be accomplished by man.

It is obvious from reading the Bible that god enjoys a good conflict that results in men taking slaves and maiming and killing one another. God will never stop something that he has spent thousands of years condoning and promoting. He apparently has nothing better to do with his time than to watch his children constantly fighting as he urges them on and encourages them. He does not hesitate to approve of capital punishment. Capital punishment will never be made immoral by god. If the "eye for an eye" concept is ever to be abolished and considered immoral, it will be done by man. It is humans who create and enforce morality for their tribes.

Morality is established to improve the communal living of humans and should have no relationship to gods or religions. In fact, one might well question whether the JCM god is moral by human standards. The great overseer seems to have derived a tremendous amount of joy pitting humans against one another.

> OK folks, listen up. This is god speaking. I command you to enter Egypt and burn the towns and villages. Rape the women. Kill all the children, the disabled, and the elderly…and do it brutally as I watch. You shall steal all their possessions. They are bad people and I love talking trash about them. Then you must return to the Promised earth that I stole for you and await my new Moral Code, which I shall inscribe in stone, lest you forget!

Thou shall have no Gods, other than
me.
Thou shall make no graven image or
likenesses.
Thou shall not take my name in vain.
Thou shall rest every seventh day.

If religious people were more moral than humanists, agnostics, and atheists, religion would be more acceptable, even if it were not based on logic and reason. However, such is not the case. Our jails are disproportionately filled with Christians as well as those of other supposedly moral religions. Divorce is higher in the Bible belt than elsewhere. Priests have a higher rate of homosexuality, child molestation, and alcoholism than most other groups. In those European countries where the majority of people are secular, there is significantly less murder, violent crime, and rape than in the United States, supposedly a nation with family values living under god's morality.

Christianity does a great deal of harm by teaching that no matter how immoral one is, all that is necessary to enter heaven is to repent and accept Jesus Christ as your savior. What thinking person could possibly believe in a religion that professes to be moral, but condones any immoral activity imaginable as long as one shows remorse afterwards and accepts Jesus and worships his father?

The concept of a person needing a higher authority to determine right from wrong in human relationships is contradictory to basic human intelligence. Does a person not realize that murder is intrinsically wrong? What about sex with a child? Stealing? If we humans need a supernatural being to tell us that blowing our neighbor away with a sawed-off shotgun is wrong, we indeed are in a bad way. Many people live a moral life without god, and create their own moral code of ethics, based on logic and reason.

Studies by Gregory S. Paul as reported in the *Journal of Religion and Society* reveal that religiosity is socially dangerous. Divorce, murder, robbery, and rape are highest in fundamental groups. There can be little doubt that fundamentalists with their absolute beliefs are a menace to society. Anyone claiming to be moral in the name of god is a person acting out of fear and not out of a sense of what is right or wrong.

As one looks objectively at religion and morality one can clearly see that religion has been and *is* interfering with the advancement of human morality. Good, kind, objective people, free from religion, should establish a moral code for a society that is ever changing as man and his universe continue to evolve. You can be sure that any sect, cult, or religion will pass laws supporting their concept of morality and their creed as soon as they have the political power to do so. One has to look no further than the U.S. Supreme Court where nary a single nontheist sits, to witness this happening. Issues such as abortion, contraception, marriage, and stem cell research are all decided on what is best for god, not what is best for mankind.

According to commonly held illusions, god has created a moral code for man. Oddly enough, man has never created a moral code for god. The gods get away with murder and mayhem, all under the delusion that god is perfect and makes no mistakes.

Since we humans are not supernatural, we cannot know about supernatural morality. We can only judge by human standards, and god does not come up to human standards of morality.

SUPERSTITION

Most religious followers think that their beliefs are true. They never stop to contemplate the ridiculousness of what they believe. There is, according to them, nothing unusual about a man walking on water, raising the dead, or turning water into wine. Likewise, they believe in a talking snake and a talking donkey. Perfectly normal – happens all the time, doesn't it? These followers cannot comprehend why others do not believe as they do. What's not to believe? A young teenage virgin gives birth to a divine son, nothing unusual about that. A violent murderer kills dozens of innocent victims and still gets into heaven for an eternal paradise simply because he believes that this divine son has saved him from his sins. For those who do not believe these unbelievable myths, an eternity of suffering and misery in hell awaits.

All religions have used this kind of arrogant conviction to brainwash folks who would otherwise have the intelligence not to believe such foolishness. They honestly think that their religion is the one true religion while everyone else's religion is nothing more than mere superstition. A quick look at religions will reveal that most of the thousands of religions, past and present, have basically the same themes and superstitions.

For example, the Aztec god of rain, Tlaloc, became angry and destroyed the world by a flood. He warned two people, Tata and Nena, of the impending disaster and instructed them to build a canoe. Sound familiar? What about the Sioux creation myth? The Great Spirit slew buffaloes and ate them on the ledge of the Red Rocks. One day a large snake crawled into the nest of a bird. The Great Spirit threw a rock at the snake, which developed into man.

There have been thousands of myths and superstitions in the world's religions describing and explaining every aspect of mankind and the universe. If there were only one true creator of the universe, surely this creator would not have allowed so many different beliefs to evolve and prosper. An all-powerful god would have set the record straight from the very beginning, not waited tens of thousands of years before getting the courage to speak up. And according to JCM dogma, this god not only spoke up but he was jealous, angry, and vengeful because so many worshiped other gods and goddesses. Whose fault is that? It is not man's fault that god waited so long to identify himself. Even when he did, he would only talk to Moses. The divine book needs a little editing. We know for certain that the universe is not 6,010 years old, although according to Bishop James Ussher, the Bible makes such a claim. Why not hire a technical adviser and make a few minor corrections? Insert 4.5 billion years as the earth's age instead of 6,010. Make the earth round and have it revolve around the sun. We realize these are just typo errors, but they are very confusing.

All religions are based on superstition. Most superstitious beliefs are harmless, but those originating from pious dogma are not. Most people have some superstitions usually due to parental or other authoritative influence. Some people worry about omens that cause bad luck and tend to avoid them like the plague, without realizing that most of these beliefs originated from religious roots. One author (CG) still remembers that his mother would throw salt over her left shoulder when it spilled. She never crossed the path of a black cat or walked under a ladder. A knock on wood would certainly bring good luck as well as finding a penny face up.

While most religious superstitions are harmless, some have become so powerful that they have destroyed man's ability to use logic and reason. Angels, witches, evil spirits, demons, and sorcerers are an obsession with present day Christians. Their belief in witchcraft originated from a few brief passages in the Bible and became the cause of one of the most horrendous acts of brutality – the killing of alleged witches.

The belief in witchcraft as mentioned in the Bible was originally benign in nature. The word translated as witch in Exodus 22:18 actually meant a priestess/oracle of a foreign god. The fanaticism of this ancient superstition increased as Christianity spread throughout Europe. Initially the witch was not considered a threat to the followers of this new, burgeoning religion. The real threat to believers who wanted to get into god's kingdom came from Satan, the prince of darkness. Since no one could actually see, touch, or feel the devil, there became a need to create humans who could carry out his work. Witches ultimately filled this role. In much the same manner that Jesus was god in the flesh, witches were the devil in the flesh. Or at least they were mortals possessed by the devil.

The witchcraft superstition remained relatively dormant during the Dark Ages. This can be attributed to the fact that the church retained total control of people's lives and thoughts, and was not threatened by outside influences that could damage its position. However, in the early fourteenth century an alleged conspiracy of Jews, Muslims, and witches was perceived by the powerful church as an attempt to undermine its very foundation. Since many people coming out of the repressive Dark Ages began to use logic and reason, an urgent need arose to squelch dissension.

With traditional Christian beliefs, men were considered superior to women. This concept was reinforced by god's own personal handbook, the Bible. Therefore, women became the central targets for the devil and his evil ways. Due to their inferiority and weakness, it was easier for Satan to enter a woman's soul than a man's. This deranged misogyny was made perfectly clear by the Catholic inquisition in 1485 when they wrote, "All wickedness is but little to the wickedness of a woman. What else is a woman but a foe of friendship....a necessary evil.... domestic danger? Women are by nature instruments of Satan." One can only wonder in amazement why modern women remain Christians.

Witches were perceived as an instrument to destroy the Christian kingdom through magic and poison. The Black Death (bubonic plague, 1347-1349) began an era in history in which panic swept through Europe. Natural disasters, disease, and other unexplainable phenomenon were now being blamed on the devil and his evil representatives, witches. For the next several hundred years it is estimated that 50,000 people were executed as convicted witches, of whom only twenty percent were male. Many more were tortured and imprisoned. The harshest period for capital punishment in the history of Europe was not due to rape, robbery, or murder. It was due solely to being convicted as a witch. The modes of execution were not the most pleasant; hanging, burning at the stake, and torture until death. The church had no moral reservations concerning the brutal killing of these humans, for it had the blessings from the divine authority in writing. Exodus 22:18 states, "You are not to permit a witch to live." What better legal grounds are there to justify mass murder than a written directive from god?

The preoccupation with this ancient superstition did not end in Europe. It traveled to the New World with the early American settlers. In Salem, Massachusetts, the Pilgrims took their obsession with witches to a new level. Although only twenty convicted witches were executed, this was a time of fanatical religious behavior. The irony of the Salem witch hunt is that the original American settlers came to the New World to escape religious persecution by the dominant church in England. The atrocities at Salem were nothing but control and persecution by the church. As unbelievable as it may seem, the first code of New England's Puritan colonies passed in 1641 stated that witchcraft was one of the twelve crimes punishable by death. It read, "If any man or woman be a witch, that is, hath consulted with a familiar spirit, he or she shall be put to death." The local courts spent as much time prosecuting witches as they spent prosecuting real criminals. A murderer fared better in Puritan Salem than a suspected witch. After all, murderers can be forgiven; a soul possessed by the devil has no redemption.

Modern Christians have not distanced themselves from an era where ancient, unbelievable superstition ruled society. They attempt to disassociate themselves from their violent past, but as long as they continue to believe in the unbelievable, they will remain permanently attached to the same folks who killed little old ladies because they were possessed by the devil. Perhaps John Adams summed it up best when commenting, "If the ancients drank wine as New Englanders drink rum and cider, it is no wonder we hear of so many possessed with devils."

Beliefs in the supernatural may have played a useful role centuries ago, but they have outlived their usefulness. People with little knowledge of themselves and their environment created their gods to explain their desperate conditions and to give hope to their future. Religion was the drug of the time and faith could cure all.

It is time to realize that religion is a deadly drug and that the addicts on heroin or cocaine are not nearly as threatening as the religious fundamentalist with plastic explosives strapped to his body.

INTOLERANCE

Humans have always had a diverse range of physical and psychological characteristics. Each and every one of us has our own unique blueprint based on these characteristics. We differ, for instance, in height and weight as well as in other characteristics such as skin, hair, and eye colors. We also differ in our psychological characteristics such as intellect, business and professional acumen, and generosity. We are born with different physical and mental abilities as well as with differing handicaps.

Given this diversity, societies label us accordingly. However, there is a downside to this labeling. People who look different from the dominant group and those who hold different beliefs are often discriminated against and treated harshly – even cruelly. Lepers were discriminated against because of their infliction; Jews were discriminated against because they were Christ killers; prostitutes because of their sexual behavior. People in these categories were harassed and looked upon with suspicion.

In this chapter we will explore how religion aids and abets the persecution of witches; how it encourages religious wars based on doctrinal differences; how it persecutes people of different races and ethnicities, as well as homosexuals, agnostics, and atheists.

Tolerance is respecting others' differences, beliefs, and practices without sharing them;

intolerance is the inability to respect and tolerate differing beliefs. Most human intolerance has resulted from religious beliefs and has been the main reason for conflict and strife throughout the world. Almost all religions brainwash believers into embracing only those who share their beliefs and ostracizing those who do not. Even members of the same religion believing in the same god have fought and killed one another because of minor doctrinal differences. The arguments and fights between liberal and orthodox Jews, between Catholics and Protestants, and between Sunnis and Shiites are examples. We still see folks arguing with one another because they cannot agree whether or not the mother Mary remained a virgin her entire life. They still argue whether one goes to hell because of a lack of good deeds or because one does not accept Jesus as one's savior. In the Middle East, Muslims and Christians are fighting and killing one another over minor variances in their beliefs, while the same god is watching over them and encouraging those atrocities. How incredulous it is that millions of human lives have been lost over petty differences. Most of the religious differences do not amount to a hill of beans.

Some Christians pride themselves in not believing in evolution. They think Darwin was an idiot for suggesting that we humans evolved from apes. For the most part, those who criticize evolution do not understand it. They do not realize that they and their beliefs are the product of evolution and adaptation. Not only does man evolve and adapt, so too does religion.

Today's Christians originated from those who had no tolerance for other religions. Baptists and Methodists evolved from the early Protestants, who evolved from the Catholics, who evolved from the Jews. The earliest Romans considered the Christians heretics and atheists because they believed in only one god. Each denomination believes that its doctrine is the only true one and that all others are false.

A close look at history reveals that all of the JCM religions evolved from a single group of religious believers, the early Jews of Abraham. The central figure in the Christian belief, Jesus, was a Jew. Moses, who personally delivered god's commandments, was a Jew. Christians originated and sustained an extreme hatred and intolerance for Jews and this hatred eventually led to the Holocaust under Hitler.

Religious intolerance is one of the biggest issues facing the world today. Anger, revenge, hatred, and killing all play a role in the inability of one person to accept another because of differences in beliefs.

Christians feel they have nothing to learn from others with different perspectives. They raise their children from birth with blinders and do not allow exposure to other beliefs. Unfortunately, small children are brainwashed and threatened at an early age with the fear of an angry god, and are taught that any dissension from god's doctrine will result in eternal punishment. They are also taught that any person not believing the dogma of their sect is evil and is going to hell. What a burden to place on a six-year old child! With this punishment hanging over a child's head, he learns to dislike everyone who is not a Christian. As the child develops into an adult, the preacher assures him that he is going to heaven as long as he continues to believe in this ridiculous superstition. Questioning is not an option, regardless of how sensible and logical the questions are.

The ugly face of religious intolerance shows itself in all facets of life. Many religions forbid marriage outside their denomination. Not believing in the same dogma is unacceptable. Millions of men and women marry those with different religious beliefs without disclosing the differences. This stay-in-the-closet attitude has been a mainstay of human relationships for thousands of years. Even in business and friendship relationships, many people choose to remain quiet or lie about their religious beliefs in order to gain acceptance and buy social peace. It is easier to go with the flow than to rock the boat. Many business deals and contracts have been won and lost because of religion. How sad it is to think that a person has to lie about a supernatural belief in order to receive a business contract. And we are in the twenty-first century!

Another major area of concern is religion in American politics. In order to be elected to a political office, a politician must profess to be a Christian, or at least a god-fearing Jew. This is true whether a person is running for town council or President of the United States. Voters have no tolerance for a candidate not believing in the supernatural. For a candidate to announce that he or she has no religious affiliation is tantamount to conceding the election even before a single vote is cast. Appealing to Christians in America is a sure way to be elected, regardless of real-life issues. George W. Bush was elected by far right Christians in 2004 because he opposed stem cell research funding and gay marriage. These are religious hot button issues and are more important than the economy, national debt, environment, and funding for education and the poor.

It is depressing that a democratic society with a separation of church and state is still choosing its leaders based on religion. President Bush has only helped to increase the mutual animosity that exists between Christianity and Islam, two of the world's largest religions.

Hitler rallied the entire German nation into accepting his hatred of the Jews, an intolerance that resulted in the annihilation of six million human beings. Today, Islamic extremists are a major world problem, but we must also realize that they are reacting to an intolerance that began over a thousand years ago with the Holy Crusades. There is no simple answer, but brainwashing Christians and Muslims to hate each other is not the solution.

President John F. Kennedy said it well, "I believe in an America where religious intolerance will someday end…where every man has the same right to attend or not attend the church of his choice." Although raised a Catholic, Kennedy had the foresight to understand the harm religious intolerance causes. As we see more people of diverse religions settling in America, we must be more aware than ever of the differences in their beliefs, and tolerate them even if we do not accept them. A truly secular presidency is not on the horizon, but as our nation and our world merge into one, the role of religion will have to be placed where it belongs – in the private homes, temples, mosques, synagogues, and churches.

Differences in the human race have also created intolerance. Most intellectuals know that race is nothing more than humans having different physical traits and as the world continues to modernize and integrate, the differences will diminish. Different physical characteristics such as skin color and body hair will no longer be required by nature to protect humans from their environment. Worldwide interbreeding will break down physical and religious barriers. Unfortunately, our history pages are soaked with blood spilled from those humans who were not recognized as equals. Race and religion have become synonymous with intolerance.

Early European explorers to the Americas looked upon the native inhabitants as inferior and subservient because of their race, customs, and religious practices. Torture, execution, and slavery became commonplace among those hapless victims. Since the Bible condoned slavery, a large number of Africans were brought to America in the eighteenth and nineteenth centuries. They were used in the most inhumane and humiliating manner to serve and work for the powerful and dominant white Christians, a fact that most Christians ignore today.

Slaves were considered substandard humans and many laws existed prohibiting their rights as equals. Even in the twenty-first century, some whites will not accept black Americans as equals. Civil rights activists such as Rosa Parks and Martin Luther King were instrumental in breaking down those racial barriers, but not without bloodshed. Sadly, there still exists an intolerance of African-Americans in many areas of the country.

Intolerance and prejudice against homosexuals runs rampant today based on biblical teachings. Leviticus 20:13 states, "If a man lies with another man...he shall surely be put to death." Leviticus also states that homosexuals *must* be killed. Whose responsibility is it to kill the homosexuals? What a hateful statement endorsed by a loving god who supposedly loves everyone. For two thousand years this biblical injunction has caused hatred and intolerance towards men and women choosing to have sexual partners of their own gender. Although homosexuals are not put to death as was demanded in Leviticus, they are the target of many religious hate groups. Homosexuality is as old as mankind itself. With religious groups making this practice a sin – discord, hatred, and persecution are thrust upon the homosexual community. Epidemics and natural disasters are blamed on homosexuals as a wrath from god. The AIDS epidemic, according to some religious zealots, is punishment from god on these sinners. Unfortunately, god's aim is not very good since newborns, children, and other innocent people are also affected by the AIDS epidemic. Many right wing religious fanatics consider the recent devastating hurricane in New Orleans a vengeful retaliation from god against all the local gays and sexual deviants. This farfetched notion resembles the Noah's flood story, except this time god decided not to kill everybody. To think, here in the twenty-first century people still believe that!

Religious intolerance has a devastating effect on life and family values. In America, most religious followers believe that a true harmonious balance in the family cannot exist without the presence and involvement of a supernatural god. They teach their children that they either worship an all-powerful god or go to hell for eternity. Sabbath is reserved for god and laws are passed prohibiting people from working on Sunday. Working on the Sabbath is a sin, although the preacher who proclaims the holiness of the Sabbath is making his living by working on that holy day. Religious people tend to ignore the fact that modern life cannot be sustained without someone working on the Sabbath. The staff and the cooks at the local restaurant, the police, firemen, doctors, pilots, NFL football players, television crews, and the plumbers are all working on the Sabbath. One can only imagine that there must be some waiver to those Sunday workers who benefit the pious. Perhaps there is a waiver that these workers can obtain to keep from going to hell, especially if their work benefits the Christians.

Deep-rooted Christians are intolerant of family members who do not share their same values. Atheists and freethinkers are forced to remain silent while the family says grace at the dinner table. Rather than make a scene, nontheists usually go along with the ritual. It is very difficult for the nonbelievers to thank a god for food when they see millions of humans starving. The believers thank god for looking after their well-being, even though a daughter or son might have been killed in an accident a week earlier. Millions of nonconforming family members go through these rituals to avoid rejection.

Many marriages break up over a difference of beliefs, resulting in broken homes, financial problems, anger, and hatred. Ironically, many children growing up in a secular family environment live full and loving lives. They are not taught to hate others and they are not threatened with eternal punishment. These children grow up realizing that they are responsible for their own actions and have no deity to blame or to praise for their success or failure.

Religion has so permeated the justice system that no one who professes to be a nonbeliever will get a fair trial. It is difficult to imagine a jury being objective and fair when judging an atheist after being taught that atheists are immoral. Most people believe that without a god to keep people straight, they become robbers, rapists, and killers. So, never refuse to put your hand on the Bible and never admit to the Christian jury that you do not believe in their god!

As long as religious intolerance remains a factor in the world, there will continue to be anger, hatred, persecution, and killing in the name of god. Religions will never come together and accept one another. That would be admitting defeat, and we humans have a difficult time doing that. Only when religious fanatics realize that there is only one world and that we all came from the same beginning, will we see harmony in human relationships.

UNINTELLIGENT DESIGN

The Darwinian approach to evolution and natural selection accepted by most scientists has been challenged by a small group of creationists who call themselves scientists. In their attempt to force all to believe in god, they have coined the term Intelligent Design (ID), which presumes an intelligent designer that has no designer. The few scientists who have been pushing ID are the same folks advocating creationism as depicted in the Old Testament.

Some who look at a glass half filled with water see the glass half full; others see it half empty. So it is with looking at nature. Some see an intelligent designer behind the wonders of nature. Others see only an evolutionary process and the adaptation of nature. Many others see the cruelties, failures, and stupidities of a designer. Let us look at the record of the designer.

It is one thing to awaken in the morning to a light blanket of snow covering the trees and the landscape, creating a picture of beauty and serenity and be in awe of nature; it is quite another to get out of bed to a seventeen inch blizzard, which blocks roads with snow and downed trees and creates great inconveniences for people. Intelligent Design?

It is one thing to be healthy, young, vigorous, economically secure, and free of pain; it is another to be old and feeble with bodily organs wearing out and in excruciating pain. That is unintelligent design. It is one thing to have a nice gentle rain, which makes your corn grow and the lawn look beautiful; it is another to see the flooding in New Orleans and a tsunami in Sri Lanka. If there is an intelligent designer, it is cruel and monstrous. In reality there is more evidence for unintelligent design than for intelligent design. The glass is not even half full.

Hospitals are filled with people with poorly designed organs. Hundreds of medical books attest to unintelligent design. Disasters such as hurricanes, floods, earthquakes, and tidal waves are called natural disasters so that an intelligent designer will not be held responsible. However, logic does not allow an all-knowing, all-powerful, supernatural designer to be called intelligent when one is faced with the cruelties of nature and the diseases in the animal kingdom. Any intelligent designer that is given credit for the wonders of nature must also accept the blame for its calamities. The existence of natural disasters and the unfairness of life prove that blind physical forces govern the universe. If there is a designer, it must be called unintelligent and cruel.

Religion has always required people to accept beliefs on faith rather than logic and reason. When a belief becomes established based on experimentation and verification, it becomes truth, not faith. Faith replaces mankind's lack of knowledge – ignorance if you will – until the premise or theory can be proved or disproved. The existence of an intelligent designer can be disproved, but only if people are willing to think reasonably and logically and are not afraid of the wrath of god. History has shown that faith decreases as knowledge increases.

The eye is often used as an example of proof for intelligent design. Many look at the eye and in their ignorance of how it works, say, "The eye is such a wonderful organ, there must be an intelligent designer behind it." Think of Helen Keller who became blind before she was two years old; tell that to a child who must wear thick lenses to see; tell that to a person with congenital abnormalities or to someone who has developed cataracts, retinal detachment, glaucoma, or macular degeneration; tell that to someone who must wear trifocals in old age.

The same poor design can be found throughout the entire animal kingdom. No omniscient, omnipotent being would design a kidney that would form a 3 to 4 millimeter stone that could block a ureter, causing excruciating pain. No woman who has suffered the pain of childbirth would design a ten-pound baby to be pushed through a narrow passageway. A recent cartoon nailed it when it showed a man with breasts and a useless appendix. The caption read, "Intelligent Design?"

The intelligent design believers think that the universe and the human body are so wonderful that they had to have been created by a god who was even more wonderful and complex, but has no creator.

Intelligent design – baloney! Any idiot could have and would have done a better job. Considering the powers that are supposedly possessed by the intelligent designer, we must leave intelligence out of it. Physicians capitalize on the failures of the intelligent designer. They realize that if there were an intelligent designer, they would be out of work. Why does god need to be perfect when he has doctors to correct his boo-boos?

The intelligent design theory is merely another attempt by religion to teach creationism and prevent the spread of truth and knowledge. As such, it deters the advancement of science and the betterment of mankind. Those pushing intelligent design are attempting to convince themselves and all others that a smart, intelligent, supernatural being created the universe and is intelligently looking after it.

The extinction of thousands of plants and animals gives proof that they were poorly designed to adapt to and survive the changing conditions of the environment. What about the dinosaurs? We know that they existed. Many have stared in awe at the skeletal remains of these mighty beasts. It has been proven that these creatures roamed the earth between 65 and 220 million years ago. That is a bit longer than when the Bible says the earth was created. Why were the dinosaurs never mentioned in Genesis, which claims the earth was formed only several thousand years ago? Why did Jesus not know about the millions of years preceding his ministry? The answer is very simple. He was not god, nor was he the son of god. Had he been god as the author of the fourth gospel attested (no other biblical authority maintained that Jesus was god) he would have known that ancient beasts existed millions of years before he was born. However, he did not have a clue. Jesus knew less about the universe than the scholars of his time. One would think that the son of an intelligent designer would make better use of his time by educating people rather than making more wine for a bunch of drunks.

A catastrophic event happened millions of years ago to eradicate the dinosaurs and most other species that existed at that time. Our scientists do not know exactly what happened, but most agree that an object hit the earth from outer space and created conditions that were not conducive to life. It took several million years for the earth to rejuvenate and form new life. Ultimately, fortunately for man, some of these new life forms evolved into humans.

We must ask, "Why would an intelligent designer allow this catastrophe to happen in the first place?" One would assume that an all knowing, all-powerful intelligent designer would not allow a meteor to strike the earth and destroy his creatures. As far as we know, dinosaurs were not capable of committing sin. Or were they? Perhaps they were zapped by god for the same reasons that humans were, millions of years later. Obviously god did not allow only the righteous dinosaurs to survive by building an ark for them. Or if he did, perhaps the boat sank. A fully grown Tyrannosaurus weighed 14,000 pounds and with his wife, kids, and their wives, a crudely built ark would have been severely overloaded. If the intelligent designer had not screwed this one up, perhaps our pets today would be purebred Apatosaurus and not tiny toy poodles.

Mankind will become extinct on the earth when the energy of the sun is used up, or when humans use their knowledge of science to alter the environment to the point where man can no longer survive. We can only speculate whether overpopulation, the development and use of weapons of mass destruction, global changes in weather and in environment, natural calamities, or the greed, bigotry, and intolerance of the human race will cause man's extinction.

Perhaps, for our personal happiness, we should take the attitude of the astronomer who said it was not really a serious concern as the earth was not a very important planet and was only one of billions in the universe. Pcrhaps god was experimenting with the earth and mankind and realized that they were both a total disaster. Since he is the one who screwed up the planet, he might have decided to go elsewhere in the universe and start anew. Who could blame him? Hopefully this intelligent designer has learned from the mistakes he made on earth. We can only hope that this time he has learned to control his temper and does not allow the devil to tempt him. If god has left us to start a new world elsewhere, man will be better off. Good riddance! Instead of spending our lives worshiping and stroking the ego of an unintelligent designer who allowed diseases, tragedies, and disasters, we might try to control our destinies and do a better job for humanity. Unfortunately, humanity will never do a good job managing its affairs as long as people continue fighting over whose god is the real god and as long as they believe that god is controlling the universe.

Intelligent design is pseudoscience and has no place in schools and public education institutions. It may be taught in religious institutions where the clergy are allowed to teach that man and the earth are the center of the universe and that a benevolent god is looking after them. However, ID should not be taught in government-sponsored public schools. Intelligent design without scientific proof is no more accurate than the Greek god Apollo driving his golden chariot across the sky to move the sun. It is no more accurate than any of the other myths concerning the creation of the universe that were held by ancient tribes. Reasonable, intelligent people will await the results of the studies being made by physicists and astronomers to discover the origin of the universe.

Forcing intelligent design to be taught in our public schools as science deters and interferes with the advancement of true scientific knowledge and the advancement of humanity. You can be certain that the church will never allow Unintelligent Design (UD) to be taught in their institutions.

HITLER

Most Christians refuse to acknowledge the rise in power of the most evil man ever to represent the Catholic Church and Christianity. The atrocities perpetrated by this despicable despot are unprecedented in recorded history. That man was Adolf Hitler.

The atrocities Hitler thrust upon the world are the most horrendous and unexplainable acts to be addressed by modern Christians. Hitler's tenure as Germany's dictator has literally been swept under the carpet and ignored by most theologians. After all, a man evil enough to perpetrate the capture, torture, and mass execution of millions of helpless human beings could not possibly be a Christian and get into heaven. But, according to Pauline Doctrine, this brutal monster is sitting in god's kingdom of heaven now and is enjoying eternal peace, while the six million Jews he annihilated are burning in hell.

There is no doubt that Hitler was a devout lifelong Catholic. He was raised a Catholic and attended Catholic schools. In his book *Mein Kampf,* numerous references are made to his religious beliefs. Prayer in schools was customary and children prayed for the welfare of Hitler and Germany while Hitler was in power.

The Jews became an obsession with Hitler at an early age, and remained so until his death. As quoted in his book, "I am convinced that I am acting as the agent of our Creator. By fighting off the Jews I am doing the Lord's work."

Hitler's anti-Semitic hatred for the Jews did not evolve from nowhere. The preaching and teaching of the Catholic and Lutheran Churches created this hatred against the "chosen people." Hitler followed suit and with the support of the Catholic Church and the Pope, rose rapidly to take over the German empire. The support of the German citizens came from their religious beliefs. Hitler convinced the masses that his campaign was the result of carrying out god's word. Had this psychopathic maniac not used religion to rally the Christians of Germany, he might have remained an obscure, insignificant, local troublemaker.

Hitler signed a concordat with the Vatican in 1933. This gave the Catholic Church financial support and in return the Church refrained from criticizing Hitler and his Nazi Government. The Vatican supported Hitler until Germany began to lose the war. Hitler was never excommunicated and the Vatican aided hundreds of Nazis to escape after the war. Nazi Germany was a fine Christian nation in the eyes of the Vatican. Christians can look forward to meeting Adolf in heaven. The Church should hang its head in shame for failing to criticize mass murder.

Hitler wore religion on his sleeve and used religion in his quest to conquer the world. Millions of Germans passively stood by and accepted his rhetorical outbursts against the Jews, Serbian Christians, and other religious sects that did not coincide with his concept of the Christian Aryan race. We should also note that Germany was in the midst of an economic depression due to the outcome of the First World War and was ostracized by the rest of the world. This made the citizens vulnerable and desperate.

Today most Germans are reluctant to discuss this embarrassing episode in their history. To be duped in the name of religion and support an evil dictator who caused the vicious and brutal deaths of millions, is obviously not something anyone should be proud of. But the truth remains that millions of German citizens blindly followed a nefarious leader sadistically driven to conquer the world under the auspices of the Christian god. We must admit that Hitler with his threat of force, like religion with its threat of hell, successfully controlled human behavior.

During World War II all commodity production focused on supporting the war rather than enhancing the lives of humans. U.S. automakers were forced to turn their attention to producing military vehicles. Consequently no new automobiles were produced for several years. European cities were devastated by bombings and cities lay in ruins. Millions of people died. The world ceased to function normally because of a leader doing "the Lord's work."

Unfortunately, the painful memories of Hitler have not changed things. Nations continue to wage war in the name of god. If we do not learn from the past, we will be condemned to repeat it. Our own U.S. President has waged a war against Iraq because god talked to him. Hitler and Bush had a direct line to the Creator and they understand what it wants. This is not surprising as the Old Testament is full of stories where god has ordered vicious attacks of one nation against another. Although people allegedly originated from the same source, Adam and Eve, they seem to want to continue to kill each other in the name of their god – the same god that supposedly created them. A brutal and murderous dictator like Hitler can have an easy access to heaven as long as he accepts Jesus Christ as his personal savior and repents.

World peace will materialize only when all humans realize that no government or nation can conduct its affairs based on the supernatural. History has repeatedly demonstrated the dangers of allowing a leader to use religion as a basis of national management. Secular administration by all nations is vital for global harmony if we are to progress toward world peace. The Founding Fathers of America realized the danger of mixing state and religion 250 years ago, but the intent and meaning of separation of church and state has somehow lost its validity. As we enter the 21st century we are increasingly witnessing an alarming influence of religion in our government and our legal system.

As a free society we cannot allow religion to control government. The world must come together as one, in the absence of god, and not allow power to those leaders who will indiscriminately kill innocent human beings in the name of religion. World governments must be separated from religion if humanity is to live together in peace and harmony.

FAMILY AND FAMILY VALUES

The family is the oldest social unit known to man. It started at the dawn of humanity when small groups of people huddled together for support, comfort, and sustenance. The basic family unit, until the development of the modern nuclear family, consisted of parents, grandparents, children, and other closely related members such as aunts, uncles, and cousins. For thousands of years, through wars, famines, floods, and catastrophes, this extended family sustained and nourished humanity.

The definition of a family has and is changing as societies evolve. Industrialization and urbanization replaced the extended family unit with the nuclear family consisting of parents and their young children. Despite these changes there has been nothing to replace small groups of people coming together in a closely-knit relationship to give comfort and support to the members of that small group. We should do everything possible to support and maintain families.

Many believe that religion is important to the family. The clergy uses that belief to continue their hold over their followers. As one evaluates that premise, one finds that it is not only untrue, but in reality religion can cause great harm to the family.

The first danger posed by religion is the brainwashing of its members – especially young children. When the family does not allow its members to think and reason logically over the existence of a supernatural being, then those members must either stop thinking critically or accept the commonly held belief. If any member of the family expresses his/her own thoughts concerning religion, which are not in agreement with the leaders of the family, he or she will be criticized, shunned, or even excluded from the family. In most families, religion, like sex, is treated as a taboo subject. Only blind acceptance or total silence is acceptable when the family leaders do not tolerate dissenting beliefs of religion. Many a scientist is nipped in the bud by such treatment. Many families have been disrupted by such bigotry and intolerance.

A day devoted to the pursuit of family activities and pleasures is worthwhile for family unity and happiness. While there may be family relationships built by going to church together, it would be more effective and pleasurable to play together with activities that the entire family can enjoy. Thus travel, picnics, entertainment activities, sporting activities – even a hike in the park – would cement family unity better than listening to a preacher rant and rave and end by telling the congregation that they are going to hell if they do not believe the dogmatic beliefs he is preaching.

Although this is not a how-to advisory book, we do know how families can be helped and supported. First, there must be a family or a group of closely-knit people who are available to nurture and sustain the young. The making of babies where such a support group is not in place must be called immoral by society. Children should not be born into a family that is not prepared for the care and education of that child. When the gods care and nurture babies and children, then and only then should the gods have any role in the decision making. Telling women what they can and cannot do with their bodies in the name of god is immoral and should not be tolerated. As the population outgrows the ability to care for people, outmoded religious sexual mores must be exposed to the scrutiny of realism. Those churches maintaining that god is responsible and cares about human life, must be seen as illogical and intolerant.

When children are repeatedly told by their parents and other adults that there is a god and he knows everything they do and think; that he is keeping score on them; that he will determine if they will go to heaven or hell after they die; that they can only be saved from hell by accepting Jesus as their savior, it is no wonder that they remain scarred for life. Those teachings should be classified as child abuse.

One of the harmful effects of religion is that it keeps people from thinking. By creating a god who is perfect, makes no mistakes, and allows no criticism, children are taught from infancy to be afraid of logic and reason. This imposes a tremendous strain on those who seem compelled to think, doubt, and reason. It prevents advancements in science, philosophy, and morality.

Religionists insist that "family values" come from god and the Bible. Nothing could be further from the truth. Biblical family values, at least those in the JCM religions, are all over the place. Their bibles reveal slavery, murder, adultery, robbery, prejudice, intolerance, the inferiority of women, and about every other vice known to man.

Honesty, kindness, charity, empathy, and the Golden Rule are human characteristics that predate the earliest gods and religions. They were necessary for the survival of the most primitive families. It is sad to report that most religions have departed from the simple, sensible rules of group behavior. They have substituted their own rules, all the time insisting that those rules came from their god and thus are absolute, timeless, and unchangeable.

Today family values stress sex, marriage, and stem cell research. Little is said about parenting and parental responsibility, but much is said about homosexuality, marriage, contraception, abortion, and stem cell research. Heterosexual love is acceptable but only within the boundaries of marriage. Homosexual love is absolutely against their god's desires. Asexual love is suspicious. Humankind has enough trouble establishing rules and laws concerning marriage and sexual activities; they do not need people demanding laws based on what god demands. Only when society removes god from the equation will society be able to establish the ever changing rules for human behavior. Most of the so-called family values of the religious right were never mentioned or known when the bibles were written. Yet the priests dogmatically insist that their god has given them direct orders concerning these issues.

Religions are missing a wonderful opportunity to improve the lot of humanity as they continue to convince people to accept their beliefs of god's demands. If the clergy would worry more about the human condition and less about the demands of an all-knowing, all-powerful, supernatural being, the world would become a better place. Family values, like morality, are ever changing and will never be timeless and absolute.

FAMILY PLANNING

One of the most harmful, immoral religious beliefs is the belief and teaching that god wants a child every time an ovum and a sperm get in close proximity. One powerful religious group does not even allow the prevention of the sperm uniting with the ovum, which would markedly decrease the number of abortions performed. The teaching that contraception is immoral is a serious threat to the welfare of humanity. Some religions teach that any action that prevents an unwanted pregnancy will cause one to spend an eternity in hell.

It is now known that more than one-half of all pregnancies end in abortions as a result of natural causes. We can only assume that nature's abortions are approved by an all-knowing, all-powerful supernatural being that is responsible for everything that happens. Since god causes so many abortions himself, he should therefore accept and approve of human-induced abortions

Though many people have predicted that overpopulation will overwhelm the earth's natural resources and food supply, no one can predict when that will occur. We are beginning to see a shortage of food in Africa, China, India, Pakistan, and parts of the Middle East. Science has improved the world's food supply by breeding better corn, wheat, soybeans, and rice as well as breeding better animals for human consumption, but there will be a time when the population is larger than the ability of science and the earth to support it.

In those countries where there is a high level of education and where families are planned and cared for, efforts to control population are working. France is experiencing an all-time low birth rate. Its citizens are educated and are living a predominantly secular lifestyle, free from religious dogma. By casting aside pious superstition, the French have taken the responsibility upon themselves in matters relating to birth control and family planning. In countries where religion dictates that sex should only be for creation and not for recreation, or where poverty and lack of education prevents contraception, the mass of humanity overwhelms their resources. Neighboring nations also suffer as political boundaries are overwhelmed with millions of starving people searching for survival. In the search for food and shelter, few rules apply and morality becomes secondary.

We frequently see groups who are actively helping the poor. Rarely do they mention the need for condoms, contraceptives, birth control, family planning, and abortions. That is not politically correct even in today's enlightenment. It is past time to face the issue of unwanted pregnancies. More people must develop the courage to speak out for family planning. Our earth cannot sustain a population based on lust and sexual pleasure.

The conflicts between the quantity-of-life and the quality-of-life advocates divide America into warring camps. The pro-life camp (actually pro-birth, with depraved indifference to the child's welfare after it is born) is based upon the sanctity of human life and god's desires. The pro-choice group, while not demeaning the value of life, is based upon human rationality and reason. It is a bitter, hate filled war with no end in sight. Only when a pregnant girl or woman is allowed to make her own decisions will this conflict cease. She should be allowed to deal with her own personal god concerning her decision.

Other than total abstinence, religion stifles any discussion of alternatives to unwanted pregnancies. Belief in the supernatural overrides science, reason, and logic. Control over the human mind continues to convince religious followers that an unchanging god makes rules on earth but does not enforce them until after their death. Only those under a paralyzing fear of god believe that all human lives have equal value no matter the age, condition, or circumstances. Only those who have been brainwashed can actually believe that a fertilized egg in a Petri dish is a child with a soul.

Nature has given the female of the species the task and the responsibility of providing the necessary environment for the development of the fertilized egg into a human being. Nature has also given mothers the primary role in the care and training of their young, even to the point of protecting them with their own lives. For anyone other than the involved female to make a decision concerning pregnancy is unconscionable.

We are not advocating giving women total control and responsibility over the conception, pregnancy, birth, and upbringing of their children. We *are* advocating giving women more freedom in the decision-making process, free from ancient, ridiculous superstition.

We cannot rely on a silent, elusive god to tell us when life begins. Apparently god is too busy starting wars to concern himself with such trivial issues. We must, as a human race, decide for ourselves when life legally begins. Intelligence and prudence tell us that a drop of semen on the sheet is not a human. Intelligence and prudence also tell us that a one-day old baby thrown into a trash dumpster *is* a human. It is up to society to determine when this transition occurs. When is it murder and when is it not? When is it moral and when is it not? If you look to god for the answers, you are only going to become more confused. God does not determine what is right or wrong for man. God killed Onan for "spilling his seed" when he refused to father a child that would be obligated to offer ancestor-worship to his dead brother rather than to himself. God then turned around and ordered all firstborn children in Egypt murdered. What a good role model! Not someone you would want babysitting your children. Unfortunately, the Roman Catholic Church took this Onan fable and ran with it. The spilling of seed anywhere but into a nubile vagina became forbidden in the church's eyes and was the basis of its birth control doctrine.

The Bible says, "All children go to heaven." If that is the case, what is the big deal about terminating the life of a newly-conceived embryo? If the church is correct in maintaining that an embryo is human life, why not go ahead and send it straight to heaven for eternity? Then the soul can be spared all the temptations awaiting it upon birth. No sex, no drugs, no wild women. The urge to steal, rob, rape, and murder will never be an issue. This lucky soul will not have the burden of deciding whether Jesus is real or not. Neither will there be the constant threat of hell while this individual plays, works, and tries to enjoy a short life on earth. One would think that, if given the choice, one would prefer to go straight to heaven before birth, rather than spending 90 short years on earth, knowing that the most minor slipup would automatically send the soul into an eternal fire pit. If the Catholic hierarchy really believed that a fetus was a human being with a soul, then the nuns in Catholic hospitals would be baptizing miscarriages.

It is hoped that god has a larger food supply in heaven than he does on earth. He has not done a good job of creating enough food for his children on earth. One can only suppose what the answer would be from a starving child in Africa if asked, "What would you rather have – no food nor shelter in miserable, scorching heat on earth, or an abundance of food inside an air-conditioned heaven?"

God may have instructed humans to "be fruitful and multiply, and replenish the earth" (Genesis 1:28), but god certainly did not tell people to multiply beyond the limits of their resources. When an omniscient, omnipotent god begins to feed, clothe, shelter, and educate the results of recreational sexual activity, then and only then should humanity listen to his views concerning family planning.

RELIGION IS CHILD ABUSE

Humans choose to organize into groups to participate in activities that are enjoyable, entertaining, and relaxing. They are social animals and yearn for acceptance and interaction with others. However, many things that mature consenting folks practice are not always in a child's best interest. Couples who want to engage in sexual activities have the right to do so, but only after they reach adulthood and develop enough maturity to understand the consequences of such behavior. Likewise, alcohol consumption, smoking, gambling, and speeding are vices that seem to consume many grownups, whether right or wrong. Most know the difference and understand the consequences of over indulgence and undue risk taking. On the other hand, a child or young person may not be mentally ready to understand these differences.

In most states it is illegal to expose children to many adult activities that could harm or impair their development. Engaging in overt sexual behavior in the presence of a child is considered detrimental to the normal development of that child and usually results in governmental intervention. Such overt sexual activities and other abusive behavior toward children are considered child abuse. Parents and other adults who abuse children are reprimanded and in some cases the child is legally removed from the home. In other cases the parents may be charged with criminal conduct.

Society has finally recognized the permanent harm caused by child abuse. What was accepted one hundred years ago is no longer tolerated today. In the old days a stern dominant father who beat his son for not working in the fields was considered a good disciplinarian and role model. After all, "spare the rod, spoil the child" was the creed for an earlier childrearing era. Today, that rod would put the father behind bars.

Modern child development psychologists realize the vulnerability of a young child's mind. A child's brain is like an empty computer awaiting any input from outside sources. Any information it receives may become embedded in that brain. The responsibility for what information is fed into children's brains rests with the parents. Parents should keep their children away from influences that harmfully affect their mental development.

Some Christian parents introduce the superstitious beliefs and fears of their religion to children before they can walk. In fact, these toddlers' first words could very well be mommy, daddy, god, and hell. Fear is instilled in their young minds at an early age and they are denied the option of questioning or challenging irrational and superstitious beliefs.

Children look at parents and clerics as the ultimate and final authority. Whatever they are told by these people in authority becomes the only truth they may ever know. The fear of the devil and his evil ways is cemented to the walls of these young cranial caverns forever. For many, it cannot be erased with reason, logic, or Clorox. Young children are forced into church on the Sabbath only to be tormented by the thunderous, resounding voice of a preacher threatening hell and damnation for all those who do not accept his teaching or his interpretation of the Bible. Graphic portrayals of the devil and his eternal prison are permanently engraved into these young minds. Some youngsters cringe during a routine church service because of the fear that is being pounded into them. All the while, the parents are smiling with glee that little junior is learning to respect and fear god.

Although Christian scholars differ in their opinion as to the age of Jesus' mother, Mary, most agree that she was very young – perhaps between twelve and fourteen years old. Why would an intelligent, all-powerful god choose a child to be the mother of his son? Surely there were other more mature virgin women available to provide this divine service. One would think a thirty-something year old would have much more stability and maturity to raise god's son than a teenage child. Maybe there were very few virgins over the age of thirteen. Regardless, a man who impregnates a young teenage girl today would find himself imprisoned for life because engaging in sex with children is considered criminal abuse. Humankind recognizes child abuse even if god did not.

Some parents teach their children that the devil is constantly watching over their daily activities. Satan, like god, knows every move they make and everything they say or do. One wrong move – zap, eternal punishment amongst the wicked; if a child lies –zap; if he steals – zap; if premarital sex occurs – double zap, with no get out of jail free card. Most parents are unaware of the torment and mental suffering experienced by children due to unfounded fear. Imagine the agony of a three-year-old girl carrying the burden of believing that an evil creature sporting a red tail, horns, and a pitchfork is constantly following her, waiting for the tiniest slip-up. This wicked guardian of the damned even knows what she is thinking.

Children growing up with religious zealots as parents learn to hate before they can walk. They are taught that people believing in something different are to be abhorred and despised. Nonbelievers are to be treated as demonic creatures that worship the devil and his evil ways. There is zero tolerance in being allowed to look at others' viewpoints because such viewpoints are said to be wrong and the work of the devil. These children are brainwashed into believing that any association with children not believing in Jesus Christ, our Lord and Savior, is a sin and punishable by the ultimate life sentence in hell. As they grow into puberty, intolerance increases into a deep personal emotion that remains permanently ingrained in their brains. Anger and intolerance become the mainstay of their thought processes during everyday activities, although most are not aware of it.

The intolerance taught to young children in church should be as illegal as torture and beatings. Why do we as a society rate movies to protect youngsters from exposure to vulgarity and adult content at the same time allowing them to be dragged into church to experience the same, if not worse? Why do we restrict minors under the age of eighteen from buying alcoholic and tobacco products? Why are minors not allowed in bars or adult bookstores? Why cannot the seventeen-year-old boy go into a topless club to look at some boobs? The answer is quite simple. He is not emotionally developed or matured to the point where he can make rational decisions regarding these indulgences. In other words, he is not ready to handle them. One would hope that as he matures, he can make his own decisions and keep these activities in perspective.

In the same fashion, young children attending a hell-fire and brimstone church service are not ready to handle what they are hearing. It causes fear and panic and distorts any hope for future reality. The members of the clergy should be held liable and accountable for the damages they are causing, just as is a child molester or abuser. Children are not mature enough to handle god and Satan. Church services should be rated according to violence, adult content, and vulgarity in order to protect unsuspecting children. One could predict that most would have the same XXX rating.

> Welcome to Hooterville Baptist Church. The Rev. Dr. Dick Byrd, pastor. Today's sermon, 'The Torture and Punishment of the Wicked.' (Caution: Adult content, violence, gore, nudity, and vulgarity) Rated: XXX!

Mel Gibson's *Passion of the Christ* is very controversial for the gore and violence it contains. Author CG sat restlessly through the movie while squirming during the obnoxious and gory scenes showing blood, guts, and torture. There is nothing in this sick movie about love, caring, and understanding. It contains more horror than any horror flick ever released. On the other hand, author JAH refused to go to the movie, not because of the blood and guts – he is used to that – but because of his frustration at seeing the multitude weep and cry over the death of someone who supposedly had the power to obtain whatever he wanted. He refused to watch a movie depicting god sitting idly by as his son is brutally tortured and crucified to prove god's love for humanity.

The most amazing aspect of this horror film is that the auditorium was filled with young children. The parents were forcing their children to watch something so cruel that it borders on the incomprehensible. The long-term effect that this movie will have on millions of hapless children will never be known. Even if this event were true and Jesus was who he claimed, why is it so important to show in graphic detail his torture and execution? Why do we have to show close-ups of iron spikes being driven through his palms? What gain is there in blood spurting out of a spear wound? Is it not enough to say that Jesus died for our sins and leave it at that? Apparently, the believers in the god of love myth think differently. Any logical person would have to wonder why Jesus, who supposedly was all-powerful, would suffer unless he desired that suffering.

A local church group decided to compete with the usual Halloween activities normally associated with children and try another approach. Instead of monsters and goblins that most children realize do not exist, the church leaders built two mockups, one depicting a scene of hell, the other of heaven. The heaven scene was spiritually comforting and displayed loving angels promoting eternal bliss. The hell scene portrayed the devil tormenting the damned and the wicked with children suffering from torture and hot burning coals. This scene was the most terrifying, horror-filled exhibit imaginable, especially for the young children who had been taken to the exhibit by their loving Christian parents. Children cried at this despicable method of demonstrating god's love. There is no doubt that many of those innocent children suffered permanent psychological damage.

Children's rights should include the right not to be subjected to the brutal methods of Christian and Muslim brainwashing. Forcing children to believe unproven myths of god, Satan, heaven, hell, and everlasting punishment by using fear and threats is child abuse. Perhaps if more fire-breathing preachers were led off the pulpit in handcuffs by the local sheriff and charged with child abuse, more children would grow up in a loving and caring world.

JESUS

The religion named for Jesus Christ has existed for two thousand years. Jesus was raised in the Jewish faith and had no intentions of creating another religion. His aim was to improve Judaism. His followers ultimately created a religion, not only separate from the Jewish faith, but in many respects, in conflict with it.

The god of Abraham, Yahweh, replaced the gods of Polytheism of earlier religions. This one and only god became the god of the Jews, Christians, and Muslims – the JCM god. The sects of the god of Abraham have fought and killed over their differences for generations.

Jesus, although upset with some of the activities of his native religion, wanted only to warn his fellow Jews of the errors of their ways. He did not make much headway in convincing his fellow Jews and were it not for Paul and Constantine, Christianity would never have flourished and spread. It would have gone the way of thousands of other religious groups that live for a short while and then die out.

Paul, a Jew by birth and training, became convinced that Jesus was the Jewish Messiah and set out to preach Christ. Although he was never able to convince his fellow Jews of that fact, he was successful convincing the uncircumcised gentiles. He was obsessed with preaching the Jewish Messiah to the gentiles and his visions and conversations with

God would be classified as psychotic by modern standards.

On the other hand, Constantine did not care what religion was practiced – he just wanted the various religious sects to stop bickering and fighting. Constantine waited until he was on his deathbed to be "saved", which seems like a good idea if you accept Pascal's wager as a legitimate reason for believing in the supernatural. ('Tis better to believe and be wrong than not to believe and be right.)

Most Christians create their own Jesus, just as they create their own god, depending upon their own morality. Good moral people create a good moral Jesus in the same manner as they create a god who is kind, generous, charitable, forgiving, and peace loving. Jesus becomes as the believers make him.

A study of what is known or written about Jesus does not lead to a Jesus like the one that many folks believe.

Jesus said that his followers would live eternally in heaven if they believed in him. If they did not, he continually threatened them with an eternity of hell. Jesus believed all of the Psalms, for he quoted them frequently and believed they were the inspired word of god. Thus he called upon the Lord God to dishonor, shame, and even kill those who were not in agreement with him. For example, in Luke 19: 27 Jesus tells a parable that ends with, "But those mine enemies, which would not that I should reign over them, bring hither, and slay them before me." Then, after telling his disciples to kill all those who did not worship him, he told them to go into the village and steal a colt as he had need of one. He instructs them,

"Go into the village opposite, where on entering you will find a colt tied, on which no one has ever sat; untie it and bring it here. If anyone asks you, 'Why are you untying it?' You shall say this, 'The Lord has need of it'" Luke 19: 30-31. How would you like that guy as a neighbor?

Jesus told his followers to turn the other cheek and to give away all of their money, but not many follow that advice. In fact, modern evangelicals seem to encourage materialism on the part of their followers – they seem to say, "If you accept Jesus he will reward you with lots of money and lots of good things."

Jesus promised to return to earth during the disciples' lifetime, not in the distant future. That did not occur, but Christians continually prepare for his return, which could be "any day now." After 2000 years with no return, one might begin to suspect that one was holding the gunnysack waiting for the snipe to jump in. When Jesus does return, apparently all hell is going to break loose for those who have not accepted him as their savior. The threats of eternal damnation with extreme pain and suffering continue to this day from the multitude of priests and clergy. Such threats not only frighten people but cause many to do harmful things in their efforts to gain favor with god. Just read any of Tim LaHaye and Jerry Jenkins' books – called end of time books – and visualize the utter violence that will be brought to unbelievers by god.

The Christian Bible does not reveal Jesus as a Prince of Peace, but a Jesus with a sword. The Prince of Peace has not been successful in bringing peace to the world. In fact, Christianity has been and is still the cause of many of the conflicts in the world today.

If Jesus really intended to die for our sins, he failed. All his suffering was in vain, for man is right back at it, sinning as much as ever. Nothing has changed in 2000 years except that more people are committing more sins. One can only imagine how awful god feels about this divine blunder. Don't fret god, we all make mistakes.

Jesus, like his heavenly father, seemed to have difficulty controlling his temper. When Jesus became upset with a fig tree that had no fruit (it was out of season) he cursed the tree and said, "Let no fruit grow on thee forever." Matt 21: 19. (Did the gospel writers ever check to see if that cursed tree ever bore fruit?)

While supposedly Jesus had the power to heal the sick, he refused to heal a sick child because she was a Gentile. The child's mother had to beg Jesus to heal the child before he consented to do so. Matt 15: 22-28. The New Testament is filled with Jesus' failures and examples of poor judgment and vengefulness.

Jesus was not a good family member and he exhorted his followers to abandon their families and follow him, just as he ignored his own parents. In Luke 14: 26 he preached, "If any one comes to me and does not hate his own father and mother… he cannot be my disciple." Jesus was disrespectful not only of his own family, but also the families of his disciples.

Men and women have created a Jesus who is supernatural and perfect, but Jesus' own words and actions contradict such a myth. For example, Jesus thought epilepsy was the result of demonic possession rather than a physical disorder.

If this god/man were perfect he would have spent his short time on earth educating man rather than causing strife and conflict wherever he went. Had he informed his followers that the earth was round and revolved around the sun, perhaps we would never have entered the Dark Ages. He could have cleared up many of the mysteries of the universe, paving the way for advanced scientific studies and medical research. While he was on earth he could have let us in on some secrets, such as how to cure cancer and how to stop a killer storm. He seemed more intent on violently turning over the moneychangers' tables at the temple. Even the act of overturning their tables was unsuccessful as some of the most powerful people in our society are money lenders, also known as bankers, many of whom are Christians.

An interesting sideline debate is, "Who killed Jesus?" Obviously the Romans were in control of the government and decreed that Jesus was to be put to death in the Roman manner of crucifixion. Although the Jews were disturbed by the rabble-rousing of Jesus and his disciples, they were not in control of the government. Jews tended to stone people to death as their form of capital punishment. Thus, Romans should be blamed for Jesus' death. However, gospel writers, in order to curry favor with the Romans, absolve them of their responsibility and turn their anger at the Jews.

Christians blame Judas for betraying Jesus. Allegedly Judas pointed out Jesus to the Roman authorities, which allowed the Romans to arrest and try Jesus. Ever since, Judas became synonymous with treachery. However, Judas, or someone like him, is absolutely necessary for the story of crucifixion, resurrection, and redemption. Jesus was predestined to suffer and die for humanity's sins. Without his suffering and death, humanity would not have been saved from god's hell. Judas should be held as god's helper. It is regrettable that Judas, and by extension all Jews, is vilified for over 2,000 years.

If Jesus had supernatural powers, then he was responsible for his own death. In that sense Jesus committed suicide. However, in the final analysis god must be held responsible. To believe that an all-knowing, all-powerful father would sit idly by as his son is tortured and killed and then claim that as proof of his love, caring, and mercy – that defies all logic and reason.

According to Christian myth, Jesus will return to earth and save 144,000 people from the wrath of his father. He wasn't successful the first time he was here but behold, he will do it the next time he shows up.

GOD'S LOVE

> Yahweh is a jealous and vengeful god. When Yahweh throws a tantrum he wreaks vengeance on his enemies and unleashed his temper against his adversaries. Yahweh is slow to anger but great in power, and he never acquits. Yahweh operates through whirlwind and storm. Clouds are the dust under his feet. He rebukes the sea and dries it up, and dries up all of the rivers. Bashan and Carmel are withered, and the cream of Lebanon curdles. The mountains quake for him, and the hills melt. The land is scorched in his presence, including the inhabited area and all who live in it. Who can stand up to his outrage? Who can survive the fury of his tantrum? His temper is unleashed like a fire, and the rocks are hurled down by him. (Nakum 1: 2-6, *The Judaeo-Christian Bible Fully Translated)*

> Yahweh is virtuous, a stronghold in the time of trouble. (Nakum 1: 7)

One would think that the most devoted of pastors would have a difficult time quoting both of those passages at the same time. Talk about speaking out of both sides of your mouth. It does not take a rocket scientist to see this ridiculous contradiction of god being jealous and vengeful on the one hand and virtuous and loving on the other. The preacher would more than likely omit the first passage and only state "The Lord is good." That won't wake the congregation.

One has only to estimate the number of innocent women and children that god has killed, as written in the Bible, to get an idea of god's love. Not to mention the innocent women and children that god ordered the Israelites to kill. Every once in a while he would tell them that they could keep the virgins for their own use. What a guy!

Many believers omit the terrible things god did and only stress that god is good – that god is love. They are very much aware of the European tendency for folks to live secular lives without superstition and fear. Many countries within the European Union have over fifty percent of their populations living happy, fulfilled lives without divine intervention. Many cathedrals are becoming tourist attractions as opposed to temples of worship. The donations they generate are used for renovations.

In the United States many of the clergy realize that to maintain membership, a facelift in Christianity is required. Modern educated people are sick and tired of the belligerent hellfire and brimstone approach of religion. The Bible is so full of ancient, antiquated beliefs that many are finally getting the courage to speak up and deny its validity.

Modern liberal preachers are downplaying the cruelty and intolerance of so many of the passages in the Bible. They are changing the stories to accommodate their congregation's needs.

> Folks, sorry about the confusion over the last 2000 years. We really didn't mean it. Just having a little fun scaring your young children…nothing wrong with a little fun, right? We have a new god now. Yep, he's reformed. Went to Counseling for Gods and came out a new man. Saw the light. He shut down hell, ran the devil off, and has promised to let up on the floods and earthquakes for the wicked. He loves everyone now…uh, well, almost everyone. He's still going to throw some AIDS at gays and some missiles at Muslims, but other than that, he's a changed man.

The problem with this new approach to god is that most of the content of the Bible must be discarded. Beginning with Genesis and ending with Revelation, the Bible would have to be totally rewritten to accommodate this new, improved god of love. Most of the passages in the Bible refer to anger, hate, jealousy, revenge, and punishment. To rewrite the Bible would imply that the church has been wrong for 2000 years. Two thousand years of punishment, torture, killing, and wars, affecting scores of millions, only to find out it was **WRONG!**

Another reason the "God is love" concept is going to be a hard sell is because many people relish the plight of nonbelievers. It makes good copy to hear the preacher yelling and screaming at those lost souls who have not found Jesus. They actually wake up when they hear all the gory details about the sinners rotting in hell while the devil is poking them with his pitchfork. Many go to church for the same reason they slow down going past a deadly automobile accident. If they look closely enough, they might just see a decapitated body. It is human nature. Take away the violence, anger, and gore from religion and "I'll just go home and watch a football game." Without such obscenities, the pews would quickly empty.

Modern clergy have a dilemma in marketing their highly profitable product – selling tickets to heaven. (Although the government allows it to be called nonprofit on the books). The problem is how to attract new investors. Do you preach a loving and peaceful god, or do you preach hellfire and damnation to keep the old timers?

One's first guess might be that violence will win out over love and peace in America's churches. After all, the old timers are more financially secure and if they are going to stuff donations in the collection plate every Sunday, they are going to want to get their money's worth. If love and peace is preached, no one need go to church.

God's love sounds good at first, a lot better than god's hate and anger. However, for a new generation of educated believers to come on board, more must question events and issues in the world that are more in line with god's anger and vengefulness. Disease, natural disasters, hunger, and human suffering cannot be caused by an omnipotent god of love.

God seems to be more concerned about obtaining love and devotion *from* man than he is in giving love and devotion *to* man. Emily Dickinson wrote in *Poems*:

> God is indeed a jealous God
> He cannot bear to say
> That we had rather not with Him
> But with each other play.

The contradictions between observing god's love and the harsh realities of life are obvious. If god loves us, he should show it. Perhaps he shudders at watching an airliner spin out of control, hitting the ground with two hundred people aboard.

> Wish I could help you folks, but I'm only god. Nothing I can do. I can't even notify your next of kin. But I love you.

As the clergy attempt to cherrypick the Bible to find a loving god, they are faced with the challenge of deciding how much power god actually has. If he causes earthquakes, famines, plagues, and other disasters, surely he can cure cancer. If he cannot stop cancer, he cannot cause a hurricane. If god does not cause hurricanes, then the Bible is wrong.

If humans want a god, they should start all over with its concept and design. They should create a god who is believable to all ranges of human intelligence. They must take anger and hate out of the same sentence as love and caring. Admit that the new god has no power over earth and its inhabitants. As the United States is on the threshold of witnessing its first female president, perhaps we should let the new god be a woman.

Although most gods are said to give unconditional love, in reality they all give conditional love. Love, like many other words, has multiple meanings. It may be a strong liking, such as the love of apple pie a la mode; a desire such as I would love to go on a cruise; devotion such as love for one's country; sexual activity such as making love; or as a strong attachment, fondness, or devotion to another person or object. Accepting the last definition of love, we can now discuss and evaluate god's love.

Many have said that god is love and that god gives unconditional love, but in the next breath they give the conditions for god's love. In Christian belief one gets god's love only on the condition that he repents his sins and accepts Jesus Christ as his lord and savior. Otherwise, the hapless soul is zapped straight to an eternity in hell. That is quite a condition! Supposedly god gave man a brain to use. Had god given people less intelligence, the gulag of the wicked would not be so overcrowded.

To scare people into doing the clergy's will by threatening them with god's vengeance is cruel, detestable, and immoral. It gives the church leaders control over their followers. If that control were used to create good, moral, loving people it might be of value, even if not true. However, when the clergy uses that control to manipulate others into doing their bidding, it is immoral. When that control is used to create laws to make people follow their dogma, it is a swindle – a fraud. As stated before, morality should be based on what is best for mankind, not what someone thinks is best for god.

For those who see the random tragedies of life and death and cannot accept the JCM biblical god, many have changed their god into a god of love. All can see that god is not simply a god of love, but is a god who sets conditions on his love – or else!

The purest form of unconditional love is the love of a mother for her offspring. Throughout the animal kingdom we see examples of the pure love of a mother for her progeny. Mothers will protect, fight, and die for their children. A loving mother does not send her child to hell, regardless of the conditions. Many children do not love their mothers in return – many do not respect their mothers. No matter what a child's feelings, most mothers still give unconditional love. God should take a few lessons from these selfless mothers. They could teach god how to love his children under all circumstances. God then would be a real mother. But wait a minute. Mortals teaching an all-powerful god about morality? Someone should!

GOD'S WRATH

The threat of what god will do to people in this life and after they die permeates almost all of the religions that exist today. It is especially true with the JCM religions. If those threats were used to make people more moral, healthier, humane, or safer, they would be more acceptable even if such a god did not exist. However, the god of the JCM religions is used by the clergy, not to mention the politicians, in a power struggle to control people's beliefs and their actions.

"If your brother, the son of your mother, or your son or your daughter, or the wife of your bosom, or your friend who is in your own soul, entices you secretly, 'let us go and serve other gods,'...you should not yield to him, nor shall your eye pity him, nor shall you spare him, nor shall you conceal him; but you shall kill him...You shall stone him to death with stones..." Deuteronomy 13: 7-11.

How anyone can believe in such a being, let alone praise, adore, and worship it is beyond the imagination of rational thinkers. We must face the fact that this god does not live up to even minimally accepted standards of human behavior. A loving god should be a role model for mankind, not one to be feared.

The JCM god is admittedly a killer. In the afterlife it is a torturer. Many believers have admitted that the Old Testament god was cruel and vengeful, but believe that the New Testament god is a god of love. They believe that god became loving and merciful by coming to earth, or by sending his son (religions are still arguing about this myth) to earth to prove god's love and devotion to the human race. We should note that Jesus, a god disguised as a mortal, did not improve the lot of humankind; he just promised that we would not go to the hell that god had created for us as long as we believed in him, and only him.

We cannot enumerate the untold times god has killed people or commanded its followers to kill. The Bible is filled with numerous such accounts, and one has only to read the Bible with intellect rather than emotion to see these examples. Many good, humane people have become agnostics and atheists by reading the Bible with their intellect rather than with fear-driven emotion.

There are many who are in awe of the universe and admit they do not understand cosmology, but they cannot abide a cruel god. Thus, they have created a god of love – an intelligent designer – to provide an explanation for the unknown mysteries of the universe. Reasonable people will admit their ignorance and await the results of future research from scientists and astronomers who constantly probe and study the unknowns of the universe. They will not accept unproven myths and superstitions. Only those who must have an immediate answer explain the universe using the myths and fables of an intelligent designer.

Irate gods inflicted punishment upon mankind with famine, earthquakes, epidemics, and AIDS. Most people today ignore such nonsense but some clergy still preach it and many of their followers still believe it. Throughout history religions have blamed natural disasters and human suffering on angry gods. The Mayan god Hurakan, the god of storms and winds, would sweep away humans in its anger. Thus the word hurricane arose. The flood concept with the drowning of multitudes is present in many religions. Even today some clergy tell us that natural disasters and diseases are the direct result of god imposing its anger on sinners. After the 1906 San Francisco earthquake and fire there was a poem:

> If, as they say, God spanked this town,
> For being much too frisky,
> Why did He burn His churches down,
> And save Hotaling's Whiskey?

God apparently decided to wipe out sinners who were drinking and copulating, but for some reason he missed his target and hit the churches, leaving the whiskey distillery intact and people still fornicating.

God's wrath, according to Franklin Graham, was used to wipe out sin in New Orleans, but again god missed his target. The sinning part of New Orleans was spared and the residential area was destroyed. God wiped out hospitals, churches, and residential areas, but left the French Quarter intact. This all-knowing, all-powerful god certainly has poor aim.

In fourteenth century Europe god sent the Black Plague to punish nonbelievers. Because of his poor aim twenty five million people, both believers and nonbelievers, were indiscriminately killed. In the past twenty-five years, our loving god has conveniently zapped twenty-five million adults and children with AIDS. Last year alone, he killed 2.8 million people, including 570,000 innocent children.

One would think an all-powerful god would have state-of-the-art laser-guided AIDS that could pinpoint only the sinners and leave the rest of us alone. Even our imperfect U.S. military has better aim with its weaponry.

Even though god is incompetent in targeting sinners on the earth, he is not through. Theologians and preachers claim that we will be subjected to even more cruelty in our afterlife. Even if we mortals survive the wrath of god with his famines, floods, hurricanes, and earthquakes in this life, we must still face the wrath of god after death. This is even more frightening as god has created a hell of eternal fire and damnation for anyone who does not accept him.

God is a torturer in the afterlife. Revelations in the New Testament and Dante's descriptions of Hell, and modern fictional works by authors such as Tim F. LaHaye and Jerry B. Jenkins emphasize the perverseness of god. All of these books gleefully tell us how the nonbelievers will be punished by god after they die.

One wonders if the concept of god's wrath is a cover for sadism on the part of theologians and the clergy. When you listen to televangelists, they seem to derive orgasmic pleasure in describing hell. This attitude of sadism is reflected in the story of Thomas Aquinas, a revered saint of the Roman Catholic Church. When asked what would be his greatest joy in heaven he replied, "To stand at the parapet walls looking down into the pits of hell and watch the writhings and hear the agonies of the damned." What a fine Christian attitude!

So what do we make of all the threats and punishments by god? If those threats were used to make people more moral, healthier, humane, or safer, they would be more acceptable even if they are extreme. First and foremost, however, the god of the JCM religions and his threats in both this life and the afterlife, give enormous power to the clergy in controlling their followers' beliefs and their actions in this life.

Just as the thug with a loaded gun at your head can get you to dance, get on your knees and pray, or get your money from you "voluntarily", so too can the preacher threatening you with an angry god. You will do anything the clergy tells you to do to keep from being zapped into hell for eternity. The only necessity is to make you believe that there is such a god and that the priest is relaying god's direct orders to you.

Most religious parents instill the fear of god in their children from birth. Children are indoctrinated in the wrath and the fear of god at a young age. They are taught to fear god and its wrath and many never get over that fear. That fear is carried forth into their adult life and affects their personal relationships, their jobs, and their happiness.

There are many laws established to prevent child abuse but it would not be politically correct to establish laws to prevent a loudmouthed, authoritative preacher from predicting hell, fire, and eternal damnation if the children do not do as the preacher says. While some complain about television and radio, others take their children to see Mel Gibson's obscene violent movie, *The Passion of the Christ.*

The concept of an angry god is the driving force behind authoritarian religions. Even the intelligent, educated, and scientifically literate people fall in line and obey the preachers just so they can avoid god's wrath in the next life.

The wrath, anger, and retribution of the JCM god are such that it is totally incomprehensible to the thinking person. How anyone can believe in such a being, let alone praise, adore, and worship it is beyond the imagination of rational thinkers. We must face the fact that this god does not live up to even minimally accepted standards of human behavior. A loving god should be a role model for mankind, not one to be feared.

Many religious people have trouble with the cruel, vengeful, angry god of the Old Testament. Therefore, they claim that the New Testament god is an improvement – he is the god of love. The New Testament god loves everybody – he loves you! The New Testament god is so loving and merciful that he came to earth, or sent his only son to earth, to prove his love and devotion for us.

But there is a catch. Jesus, a god disguised as a mortal, did not improve the lot of human kind; he just promised that we would not go to hell as long as we believed in him – and only him. So much for a loving god!

For Christians, Jesus provides an easy way out. Live any way you choose, but be sure to repent and accept Jesus as your savior before you die. You are then home free to spend an eternity in a heaven that no one can describe. You can even emulate Constantine who waited until he was on his deathbed to be baptized. (Forgiveness by confession did not yet exist.) Why give up years of partying and sinning when you do not have to? Confess just before you die.

We will have to work hard to wean people from the fear of god.

First and foremost, people need to understand that the gods of the various religions are cruel and should be denounced and condemned for their cruelty. The god of the Old Testament puts modern day monsters such as Hitler and Stalin to shame. A cruel god who repeatedly engages in genocide should not be worshiped. If such acts of cruelty were carried out by modern governments, there would be a clamor to bring those governments to justice.

We need to understand the psychological damage our preachers do to children with their terrifying and gory stories of hell and god's punishments. We have many laws which are designed to prevent child abuse and we should extend those laws to prevent the loudmouthed, authoritarian preachers from talking about hell, fire, and eternal damnation to children. Just as we rate our movie and television programs to identify those that are suitable for viewing by children, we should rate the preachers – "H" for Hell and Damnation. We should make sure that children are not exposed to those preachers. It is astonishing that we complain about television and radio programs while allowing children to see *The Passion of the Christ.*

Man uses religions and gods rather than science to explain the unknowns and the realities of life. We now know that natural disasters such as hurricanes, tsunamis, and earthquakes are not caused by god's anger but by natural phenomena. At the present time we do not have the knowledge to predict when an earthquake will strike, but we know enough that it will be likely to strike within a certain period and at a certain place. The earthquake will strike whether we are good, bad, believe in god, or pray earnestly. We must counter religions' primary weapon – **FEAR** – fear of life, fear of death, and fear of god – by developing rational skills and giving up superstition, myth, and pious folklore.

Charles Darwin, as he approached death, was not afraid to die. Darwin did not fear death and damnation as he refused to take seriously Christian beliefs that were so sadistic. He wrote, "I can indeed hardly see how anyone ought to wish Christianity to be true: for if so the plain language of the text seems to show that those who do not believe, and this would include my Father, Brother, and almost all my best friends, will be everlastingly punished. And this is a damnable doctrine." God's wrath is damnable.

If we cannot get a god at least as good as a good person, we are better off without one.

GOD'S COMMANDMENTS

Jews, Christians, and Muslims have handpicked god's laws from their holy texts since they were first written. They exclude or ignore those commandments that reveal a god that is a cruel and spiteful killer, and responsible for torturing people for an eternity after death.

Most people realize and agree with the wisdom of our parents and other good people when they teach kindness, charity, tolerance, and the Golden Rule. These are virtues that we learn sitting on our parents' knees and in kindergarten. They have no relationship to a deity. Don't fight; share; don't lie; be careful crossing the street; don't jump from high places; treat others as you would like to be treated; put your toys away; don't litter; be kind to animals; brush your teeth; take care of your body and the environment. These commandments have been known and emphasized by good parents and teachers for generations. These rules of behavior were established to allow groups of humans to come together in peace and harmony.

Most Christians who preach the morality of the Ten Commandments do not realize that this set of god's laws are not actually the laws god allegedly gave to Moses in the form of stone tablets. Exodus 20, the most widely accepted reference to the Ten Commandments, does not end with only ten laws. It continues through Exodus 21, 22, and 23 and contains scores of additional commandments from god. Other books of the Bible contain hundreds of additional rules decreed by god. In fact, Orthodox Jews count 613 commandments in the Bible. One can clearly see why Christians conveniently exclude some of these rules from the courtroom walls, as they are cruel and ridiculous.

Now we shall list some of god's commandments that will not be placed on public walls:

- It is permissible to own slaves. Leviticus 25: 44-46 Exodus 21: 2-6
- Rape is acceptable. Deuteronomy 20: 10-14
- Women will not be allowed to teach, or to usurp authority over men. They must be silent. I Timothy 2: 12
- No female priests – The Bible says so.
- Cannibalism is OK. Deuteronomy 28: 53
- You are to be killed if you hit your father or mother. Exodus 21: 15
- If you curse your parents you are to be killed. Exodus 21: 17
- It's an eye for an eye, tooth for tooth, hand for hand, and foot for foot. You are to have no pity. Exodus 21: 23-25 Leviticus 24: 17-20 Deuteronomy 19: 21
- Kill all witches. The Bible says they exist. Exodus 22: 18
- If you work on the Sabbath, even if you only pick up sticks or kindle a fire, you must be put to death. Exodus 31: 14-15 Exodus 35: 2-3 Numbers 15: 32-36
- Homosexuals, even if you are born with that trait, you are dead meat. Leviticus 20: 13

- Sons who are stubborn and rebellious will be stoned to death. (Daughters seem to get off a little easier here.) Deuteronomy 21: 18-21
- Now you girls get it. If you are not a virgin when you get married you will be stoned to death at your father's door. Deuteronomy 22: 20-2
- A man having sex with another man's wife is to be put to death, as well as the wife. Deuteronomy 22: 22
- Ladies, beware; don't grab the private parts of any man fighting with your husband. If you do your hand will be cut off. Deuteronomy 25: 11-12. You won't be pitied either.
- Ladies do not have sex with a beast, lest both you and your favorite dog be killed. Leviticus 20: 16
- Girls, do not dote on your lovers who have a penis as large as an ass and an emission like that of a horse. Ezekiel 23: 20
- Fortune-tellers beware. You will be stoned to death if you receive messages from the dead. Leviticus 20: 27
- God does not want you to curse him or listen to any other gods. If you worship any other gods you are to be killed. Leviticus 24: 16 Deuteronomy 17: 2-7 Deuteronomy 18: 20. Fortunately it takes two witnesses to convict you.
- Don't forget to have your son circumcised when he is eight days old. Genesis 17: 12 Leviticus 12: 13

- When someone takes what is yours, do not ask for it back. Luke 6: 30
- Give away everything you own. Otherwise you cannot be my disciple. Luke 14: 33
- Hate your father, mother, wife, children, brothers, sisters, and yourself. Luke 14: 26
- If someone sues you for your shirt, let him have your coat as well. Matthew 5: 39

Imagine the confusion, laughter, and disorder that would be generated in our courtrooms and classrooms as judges, juries, and children read these commandments and attempt to apply them to their lives. These laws would have seemed barbaric even to the gunslingers of the Wild West.

Apparently, giving Moses these hundreds of rules for man to live by was not good enough for god. He also demanded that the people of Israel bring him offerings of gold, silver, bronze, blue cloth, purple cloth, scarlet cloth, fine-twined linen, goat hair, and goatskin. Let us put this in perspective; god created the earth in six days. That means he created gold, silver, bronze, and goats. Then he demands that man give him these things back as an offering. What can god possibly do with goat hair in heaven?

God's commandments that are stressed today are more about sexual behavior, family planning, and medical research. Our religious, judicial, and political leaders cherry pick portions of these ancient rules to create new rules that enhance their own personal religious and political agendas.

It is our misfortune that we continue to allow our leaders to manipulate people with ancient superstition.

The Old Testament, the New Testament, and the Qur'an are filled with ridiculous, inane, cruel, and inhumane instructions. It is incomprehensible how anyone can read the Bible with intelligence and come to the conclusion that it is the word of a perfect and loving god. Only those terrified of being sent to hell for an eternity by a cruel god could possibly believe and tolerate such superstition.

SAINT LUCIFER

All religions have used the theme of evil and wickedness to promote their agendas. The good guy/bad guy concept has been a mainstay of human psychology since man quit walking on his forelegs. It permeates our lives. We like a good cops-and-robbers story. Every movie has its bad guy who represents evil and keeps us riveted in our seats until the good guy finally blows him away with a .44 magnum. In fantasy, good prevails and evil loses. Political rulers and religious leaders have pitted human beings against each other by labeling some people good guys and others bad guys. This is a powerful technique to divide and conquer.

The JCM god has effectively used this divide-and-conquer approach. At the onset, the Bible divided humans into two categories, us and them, good and evil, and this remains the controlling method in these religions today. The clergy have driven a sharp wedge between people considered good and those considered bad. Using the Bible as a reference, evil has manifested itself into many different forms. Folks with leprosy, nervous disorders, and other ailments were considered bad people. This category also included prostitutes, liars, and thieves. As if these were not enough to hate, others were created. Witches, sorcerers, and fortunetellers became a part of the evildoers, even though they never existed. Entire countries and civilizations were evil because they worshiped a different god.

Like any group or organization evildoers needed a leader, someone in charge – or perhaps more accurately, someone to blame. Enter St. Lucifer, the bad guy of bad guys. This Prince of Darkness, Satan if you will, has been in charge of hell for longer than Castro has ruled Cuba. Also known as the Devil, this master of deceit has captured the imagination and fantasy of religious folks for centuries. The concept of a supernatural bad boy originated a thousand years before Jesus. The much earlier monotheistic religion of Zoroastrianism had its own devil, Angra Mainyu, the evil spirit of violence and death. He created cosmic conflict in humans as to whom to follow, the good guy or him.

Throughout history, most if not all religions have had their version of the Bad Guy in the sky or deep in the bowels of the earth. (We're not quite sure where hell is.) All of the so-called primitive native tribes had evil spirits that were constantly wreaking havoc on poor, innocent mortals. Some of these holy devils could be pacified by sacrifice of one's firstborn son or daughter, or donations via the clergy. Many of the gods stayed angry, no matter what humans did to soothe them.

The concept of the devil in the JCM tradition seems to have originated when god admitted that he created evil. Since he created evil, apparently he felt the need for a Minister of Evil, someone who could oversee the Department of Evil. Why would a loving, caring, all-powerful god consider creating more problems on earth than even he could handle? Why not spend the time and energy on making man moral and getting food supplies to the world's hungry children? Perhaps cure a few diseases when he runs out of things to do?

One can only assume that god wanted a hatchet man – one who could take the blame for all of his unintelligent boo-boos. Nothing wrong with a good hatchet man. After all, if our president can have them, god should be able to have one. Enter the fall guy, Lucifer, created by god but to be held responsible for all the wickedness, sin, and mischievous behavior in the world. Now when mortal man commits a little wickedness he can say, "The Devil made me do it." When evil occurs, god can say, "It's not me responsible; it's that bad old Lucifer."

It must take a lot of celestial effort to build an underworld prison for the wicked. How many times has it been renovated and expanded? After all, when god built this diabolical slammer for the degenerates, there were not that many inmates to keep up with. Considering the billions and billions of hapless souls who could not quite make it through the Pearly Gates over the last several thousand years, one would think the phrase "prison overcrowding" would be an understatement. What a lucrative contract to have for a general contractor – an on-going expansion program for the largest facility in the universe – eternally. Could it be possible that all these folks burning in hell are responsible for global warming? We must not let the environmentalists know that god might be responsible for global warming.

Although Lucifer is considered the epitome of evil, no single being, divine or mortal, has ever caused as much widespread destruction and ruin as god. God is the one who must take full responsibility for plagues, diseases, and disasters. He is the one who flooded the world and killed everyone except Noah and his righteous family. He is the vengeful one who ruthlessly punishes nonbelievers. He is insanely jealous. He is constantly angry and holds grudges unlike any mortal. Cross his path and look out! But when a little evil occurs, poor Lucifer gets the blame. Maybe the pious are on to something here when they say "Intelligent Creator" as the creator has rigged it so he gets all the credit for the good things that happen but takes no blame for the bad.

Religious authorities insist god does not have the power to make man good, that only man can make himself good. But, the devil has the power to make man evil. What kind of intelligent design is that? An all-powerful, all-knowing intelligent creator who created himself (yeah, right) actually created his subordinate archrival with more power than himself. Talk about a **divine** goof! Now we have an out-of-control evil world with all the wicked being controlled by Lucifer, who was created by god. To add insult to injury, god does not have the power to do anything about it but to sit on his Big Throne and stay mad. God must be busy keeping score.

> Boy, did I ever screw this one up! I created the devil to add a little excitement and naughtiness to my otherwise boring world and look what happens…he takes over. And that was dumb of me to create more power in him than I have. I've allowed him to enter the souls of man and take control

> when I can't even do that myself. I sure wish I had a daddy to call on to help. But, as we all know, I created myself and don't have a daddy.

God is very jealous of Satan. Perhaps it just kills him to see his own creation having a little fun while he is preoccupied with killing, maiming, torturing, and punishing his nonbelieving humans. God is busy being angry with everybody since nothing seems to be going his way. People just won't obey his vague directives.

Of course god has caused most of his own problems concerning his nemesis, Lucifer. On numerous occasions god has allowed the devil's boyish charm to persuade him to do something he did not want to do. In the Book of Job, god changes his mind due to this demonic insistence and inflicts punishment on poor old hapless Job, even though Job is a devout and righteous man. Wait a minute! Who's really in charge here? Who is calling the shots? This is the same god who punishes us for allowing the Prince of Darkness to change our minds. Since god created St. Lucifer, god is responsible for evil.

The devil and his evil ways are very important ingredients in the JCM religions. The clergy use good and evil to control the minds of their gullible followers. In the United States the words nigger, faggot, and atheist are words still used by Christians. They think the word atheist is a synonym for evil. This widespread prejudice against other people begins in the pulpit and often ends with the harm or death of innocent human beings. The relentless preaching of hell, fire, and brimstone by loud mouthed emotional pastors only incites deeper and deeper anger in the congregation. People become convinced that Satan and his demonic elves have entered into the souls of everyone around them, making them the enemy.

Some churches such as the Unitarian Universalist, promote fellowship among all people regardless of their race, beliefs, or sexual orientation. The ancient devil and his supernatural evil powers have no place in these modern, caring churches. Everyone is welcome – everyone feels welcomed. Perhaps more should attend a few of these services. Maybe some might leave with a feeling of kindness for all human beings.

THE DEVIL GETS A BUM RAP

Let us shed a few tears and empathize with the devil – Satan – Saint Lucifer – Beelzebub – monster – beast – demon – netherworld deity – or any of the other terms for the patron saint of evil. Most of the religions of the world have created an evil semi-god, or an evil spirit in an attempt to account for god's failures. Since the JCM religions created not only an all-knowing, all-powerful god but also a perfect god, they had to find a way to explain the disasters and calamities of nature as well as to explain the existence of evil in this world and the terrible things that happen to man.

Thus the JCM religions have a need for a lesser god who can take the blame for the more powerful god. Therefore Satan is created, a semi-deity with just enough power to cause mischief but not enough power to challenge god, to take responsibility for the existence of evil. The all-powerful god, thus, is relieved of all responsibility for evil and now has a ready-made fall guy.

The truth is that God, according to theology, is the boss of this universe and is therefore responsible for both Satan and evil. To explain the presence of evil and why terrible things happen even to good people, religious believers resort to explanations such as, "God works in mysterious ways; God is perfect so he/she/it must have something better in mind later on; God is testing you; God is strengthening you; this is for your own good; God is so smart and you are so dumb that you cannot comprehend the perfection of God."

But these explanations are obviously inadequate. They are illogical because we do not know whether the bad things that happen to people are being inflicted by god or satan and we do not know how to determine who is really responsible for those bad things. They are unreasonable because god is the only being who, in theory, has the power to foresee and stop wars, genocides, and massive disasters. During the twentieth century god seemed to sit back and watch while humans were engaged in world wars, holocausts, and other evil acts. Likewise, god is the only one who has the power to "uncreate" Satan. God should emulate Bill Cosby's oft-repeated admonition; "I brought you into this world and I can take you out!"

Then there is the belief that god is watching you and recording everything you do and at the end of your short life he will tally the score and decide whether to let you into heaven or send you to hell for eternity.

The only purpose of our life, it seems, is to run through a booby-trapped obstacle course riddled with temptations of sin. The longer one lives, the greater the chances of committing acts of sin and thus being zapped by god. According to this belief, young children are fortunate to die young and avoid the possibility of eternal damnation.

In any case, look at the issue of eternal damnation from another angle. Mathematicians tell us that any number, even one hundred years of life, approaches zero when compared to eternity (that is, infinity). That means we will be punished for an infinite amount of time for being alive for such a brief time – less than a second on that scale of time. Doesn't it seem that the punishment is disproportional to the crime? Even our imperfect legal system has a better sense of proportion between crime and punishment!

The lesser deity, the devil, according to the commonly accepted belief of the JCM religions, did not have the power to create a heaven or a hell. In addition, Satan does not determine who gets into heaven and who gets fried. Only god, not Muhammad or Jesus, determines who gets the ticket that allows entrance through the pearly gates and on to the gold-paved streets of heaven. But Satan gets a bum rap for everything that goes wrong. What a deal!

Mr. Satan, please forgive us humans for blaming you for the evils of the world that you did not create. We apologize for libeling and slandering you. Like all of us, according to the mythology of religion, you are the creation of god. You did not ask to be here – we did not ask to be here – it was god's idea. It is not you who controls the admission into hell – you just run the joint. You are only doing the job that god assigned to you. We must respect your persistence, your hard work, your dependability, and your reliability to get the job done. God gave you some good traits and we should respect them. It is obvious that this all-knowing god knew you were going to be one bad fellow when he created you, yet he set you free to wreak havoc on the human race. Reason and logic does not allow an all-powerful, all-knowing supernatural being to escape the responsibility for both evil and good. Satan is taking a bum rap.

Or, did god make you too powerful and you ousted him in the beginning as Mark Twain suggested? If you did, let us know and we will begin worshiping you. Twain also noted, "All religions issue Bibles against Satan, and say the most injurious things against him, but we never hear his side."

SPIRITUALITY

One frequently hears people say, "I am not religious, but I am spiritual." What they are really saying is that they do not believe in the myths and superstitions about eternal life, god, Jesus, or any other supernatural being but they are not willing to admit that they are agnostic or atheistic.

The authors confess to having considerable ignorance concerning spirituality, other than it being the result of actions, reactions, and functions of that human computer we call the brain. There is a tremendous amount of ignorance concerning the human brain's thinking and reasoning abilities as well as its ability to synthesize thoughts, feelings, and emotions. The brain is able to accept information that it takes in by means of our six senses and is able to react to those stimuli.

While most are familiar with Aristotle's five senses of sight, hearing, smell, taste, and touch, few are familiar with a postulated sixth sense – proprioception. Proprioception is the knowledge of the position of the body as related to its surroundings. For example, with the eyes shut in a quiet dark room, we know the position of our arms and legs when they are raised or lowered in relation to the rest of the body. In one sense this could be called feeling or touch, but in reality it does not depend upon touch – thus another sense – proprioception.

Our brain, a very complicated computer, not only has the power to synthesize the input of the senses, but it also has the power to order the various parts of the body to act and react. When the brain obtains the input from that action, the results are more action and reaction ad infinitum. In that way we learn and relearn.

There is a large amount of medical and scientific research being conducted to understand the brain's actions and functions. We patiently await the results of this research that will ultimately allow us to understand spirituality, love, and hate, as well as other feelings and emotions. While we easily understand the need to satisfy hunger, sexual urges, and physical comfort, we are further from understanding our feelings and emotions. That knowledge will come as science continues to study the brain and its functions.

Spirituality is one of those feelings that vary from person to person. In most instances the term is used by people who have recognized the foolishness of religious dogma but do not want to admit a disbelief in a god. Spiritual people usually feel they are keeping their ace card in their back pocket – just in case. Just in case there is a hell; just in case there is an authoritative disciplinarian who will put us there. Why take a chance? They do not attend church, they do not pray, and they generally do not participate in the dogmatic rituals of religion. It is not uncommon for people who are spiritual to cut their grass on Sunday morning. However, if anyone were to challenge them for working on the Sabbath, they could answer, "I am not religious but I am spiritual."

Many people are in awe, even humbled, by their lack of knowledge concerning their body, the universe, and their feelings. Einstein who was in awe of nature and humbled by the forces that he did not understand, felt a cosmic awareness that many interpreted as a belief in god. But spiritual people – people who are in awe of nature and its wonders and recognize their vast ignorance of the universe – are not religious and make no claim to be. They do not believe in the myths, superstitions, and the downright lies that religions teach and preach.

Just as many are in awe of nature as it sustains us, we must also be in awe of the same nature that kills us. The forces of nature are neither evil nor good. They simply exist. And so it is with the universe, energy, motion, gravity, and man – they simply exist. To explain the mystery of nature with the mystery of god explains nothing. It is a cop-out for human ignorance. It would be better to confess our ignorance and seek or await truth.

While ignorance is not a sin and is nothing to be ashamed of, stupidity is another matter. Those who are unwilling to think, reason, and search for truth are either stupid, lazy, or frightened of a monster that has created an infinity of suffering for all who do not believe in it. It is better to admit our ignorance and strive to get at the truth, rather than lump all of our ignorance onto an imaginary playmate in the sky.

THE SABBATH

One of the many claims in the JCM Bible states that god rested on the seventh day. Apparently, god is not as all-powerful as we are led to believe in the scriptures. After all, mortal men and women routinely work more than six days straight and seem to do just fine. Creating the entire universe in six days must have taken a lot of energy out of god. Besides, god had to deal with that annoying imperfect creature called man. That's enough to make one tired.

God seems to have needed a rest on the seventh day, a day we now call the Sabbath. Some religions claim Saturday as the Sabbath while others claim Sunday. An all-powerful, all-knowing god can not even communicate this simple bit of information to the masses. For this discussion, we will use Sunday as the Sabbath, even though sabbath is Hebrew for seventh. The seventh day is Saturday. Sunday is the day that Constantine "seventhed" when he switched from the sun-god Mithra to Jesus and brought the sun-god's sacred rest day with him.

The issue of resting versus working on Sunday has caused thousands of antiquated laws to be written by all of our fifty states – based solely on religion. This practice of writing religious laws into secular law is in direct contradiction to the intentions of our forefathers who tried to keep church and state separated. Apparently the Christians interpreted it in a different manner.

> Sure, we believe in freedom of religion. We think one should have the right to believe in any religion he chooses – as long as it is Catholic, Baptist, or Methodist. And we also expect you to follow God's Laws because we intend to use them to make the laws of the U.S. After all, as you well know, this is a Christian nation under God. Since God hasn't written his laws for us to understand them, and since he doesn't seem to enforce them, we will do it for him.

Our federal and state legislators have interpreted the Constitution in the same manner since many ridiculously stupid blue laws, based on Christianity, are still on the books. More Christian laws are written into our legislation than all of the other religions combined. One would be hard pressed to find a law that promotes Judaism, Islam, Hinduism, Buddhism, or Shintoism. Yet these religions include millions of honest, hardworking, taxpaying citizens who are required to abide by the Christian laws. Thomas Jefferson must be rolling over in his grave!

The over-zealous religious folks began integrating god's law into man's law as soon as they stepped off the ship at Plymouth Rock. Most of these Christian laws originated from the New England Puritans in the seventeenth century and many are still in effect today. The term blue law came to be applied to laws that pertained to activities on Sunday that were considered strictly forbidden by scriptures. If you happened to live in the Colony of Connecticut in the mid 1600s, you would have been required to abide by the Code of 1650. Some of those rules were:

- No one shall run on the Sabbath, or walk in his garden.
- No one shall travel, cook, make beds, sweep house, cut hair, or shave on the Sabbath.
- No woman shall kiss her child on the Sabbath.
- No one shall vote unless he becomes a member of an approved Church.

The original New England blue laws were created to force people into church on Sunday. The rationale was that if a family could not go shopping, clean house, or get a haircut, they would go to church because they had nothing else better to do. One could assume they would put a little money in the collection plate while they were there. What a great setup for the church.

Some of the penalties for breaching the Sabbath included whippings, fines, burnt tongues, and severed ears. Many people were punished for the simple crime of not going to church. These same folks spent much of their time seeking out and punishing backsliders and witches. Sadly, 350 years later this state of mind still persists.

Blue laws are obnoxious deprivations of liberty and freedom. They are the direct result of religious beliefs. Many blue laws of the seventeenth century remained on the legal books for hundreds of years. Some remain in place today. Although these antiquated laws are gradually disappearing in America, it will be a long time before Sunday is considered like any other day of the week. Most of us can still remember when it was illegal for a local retailer to sell any product other than food or medicine on Sunday. If you were working on your car and needed a part, that's tough luck. If you needed a new pair of shoes in order to start that new job on Monday, you could not get them.

Nineteen states still have some form of the blue laws in effect. For example, Bergen County, New Jersey continues to ban all forms of selling on Sunday, except food. Ironically, this area is one of the largest and most popular shopping hubs of metropolitan New York and a large percentage of the citizens are Jews or Muslims, who do not consider Sunday their Sabbath.

Alcohol is another topic for discussion. Some die-hard Christians think that drinking alcohol is a sin, although many drink when no one is looking. Millions of these pious folks condemn the drinking of alcohol, only to go home and grab a little hooch from their secret stash. What is the big deal with spirits? Drinking beverages that make one happy is as old as civilization. For those who read the Bible, alcohol was prevalent in biblical days. Wine was the drink of choice, not coffee, Coke, or bottled water. If alcohol was commonplace in biblical times, what has changed that makes current worshipers so adamant against it that they make laws that restrict Sunday sales? Currently 31 states prohibit the sale of alcohol on Sunday.

Blue laws are anachronistic in modern times. Jews who follow their Sabbath do ridiculous things to follow the letter of the law. For instance, some Jews hire non-Jews to turn on the lights and do other chores. Obviously it is permissible for non-Jews to violate the Sabbath laws and go to hell as long as they protect Jews from such a fate. In addition, in our global village, to keep the economy and trade humming and to keep society functioning properly, we need someone somewhere working all hours of the day and all hours of the night, seven days a week. We need doctors and nurses to attend to us when we are sick. Sickness doesn't care about god's day of rest. Our corporations outsource manufacturing to countries like India and China and their employees are working on our Sabbath day and vice versa.

Sabbath is no longer a feasible concept. Blue laws should have been declared unconstitutional years ago.

THE BIG SCAM

We encounter many scams as we go through life. Tricksters have tried every approach imaginable to fraudulently pick the pockets of the unsuspecting. Insurance, real estate, and investment scams are just a few ways used by con artists to siphon our hard earned money from our bank accounts. Fortunately, as we get older and wiser, most of us become more aware and distrusting of deals that seem too good to be true.

Experience, logic, reason, and prudence dictate that we investigate the legitimacy of propositions before making investment decisions and coughing up our money. Laws are enacted to protect the public from illegal scams and business ventures. Investment brokers, bankers, real estate agents, and insurance agents must be licensed by the government before selling their wares. Their daily transactions are closely monitored and continually scrutinized. They also are required to pay taxes.

For those of us who occasionally fall prey to the slick salesman selling us prime oceanfront property in the middle of the Everglades, there is recourse. We can seek legal remedy through lawsuits and the court system. In many instances, the con man is criminally charged and convicted. Even if we cannot get our money back, we can at least help take one more crook off the street.

Companies dealing in real estate and investments are not only required to be licensed, but are required to provide accurate and detailed information regarding their product. For example, a brokerage firm selling mutual funds or stocks is required to provide a prospectus outlining the pros and cons of the investments. The potential risks as well as the potential gains must be fully disclosed in order for the investor to make a rational decision.

The powerful church and its leaders, unfortunately, are not held to the same high standards of accountability. They have successfully orchestrated the biggest scam ever known to mankind. Evangelists have free rein to sell and profit from the granddaddy of all investment scams – the afterlife. The Securities Exchange Commission does not license these pious con artists. They do not have to be licensed real estate agents. They do not even have to provide a prospectus to potential investors. Our television networks allow these pickpockets to sell their wares on national TV while the government turns its head on these tax-exempt thieves, under the guise of freedom of religion. The Internal Revenue Service reported that eighty-eight billion dollars of tax free money was donated to churches last year.

The bill of goods the clergy sells to its unsuspecting victims does not come with a deed or certificate of authenticity. There is absolutely no feedback from the millions of previous investors whom the clergy insist have already cashed in on their divine reward. One would think a prudent investor would insist on additional information before deciding to commit his money and his life to this questionable investment. But the clerical scammers offer no guarantees. H.L. Mencken wrote, "A church is a place in which gentlemen who have never been to heaven brag about it to persons who will never get there."

> Trust me! Give me your money, come to church and put more money in the basket, and don't forget to send in your annual tax-exempt contribution at the end of the year. In return, I promise – trust me – you will get an eternal seat at Jesus' right hand after you croak, uh, I mean, when you join the dearly departed. Oh yeah, don't forget that you can pay for absolutions, baptisms, weddings, burials, even indulgences, with tax free money.

Imagine for a moment a person who spends a lifetime paying into this scam. He has attended church services every Sunday and Wednesday since he was a toddler. He gave up many enjoyable activities such as fishing and ball games in order to meet his contractual obligations for an afterlife. Instead of canoeing with his son, he spends his time in church praying to god to save his soul in the hereafter. He has forgone family vacations in order to pay the church the ransom it demands to keep his contract with god from becoming null and void. Suddenly, out of nowhere, there appears a loaded dump truck, ramming him head on, and then – lights out!

Not to worry, he has paid his insurance in full. He can now cash in on this wonderful afterlife that he was promised. However, when he gets to the Pearly Gates, he begins to smell a rat – there is nobody there – nothing.

> Just dark, damp, and cold empty space – nothingness. Hey, wait a minute! Where are the beautiful angels that are supposed to greet me and feed me grapes? Where is my oceanfront air-conditioned condo overlooking the glorious kingdom of god? No answer! Hey, I've been hoodwinked, bamboozled, shanghaied! It's not fair. I want a refund. I'm calling my lawyer. What? I can't? I'm dead? But I gave all my earthly possessions for a divine piece of real estate. The preacher swore to me…What? He lied? I'll kill the bastard! Too late. Just so happens that good ole Pastor Byrd is having dinner with your grieving widow tonight, uh, to comfort her, of course!

What would you think if you read this ad in the newspaper?

> For sale: Large oceanfront lots in heaven. Beautiful setting. Ideal weather. Good neighbors. All pleasurable amenities nearby. Only $5,000. Available immediately upon death. If not abso-

> lutely satisfied, your money will be promptly refunded. Contact seller for more information.

Now let us look at the one given every Sabbath in your church.

> For Sale: Tickets to heaven. Don't miss out on an eternity of health and happiness after your worldly body gives up the ghost. Simple directions. You must only believe in ______(Name your god) and pay 10% of your annual income before taxes. This allows one ticket to heaven. No guarantees. God works in mysterious ways. P.S. If you do not accept this offer you will be sentenced to hell where you will suffer for an eternity. That is guaranteed!

Millions of people continue to answer this ad even though common sense and logic show it to be pure hype. Endless amounts of time, energy, and money are spent to convince all to support their church and clergy, all the while diverting this effort from helping humanity. Just think what might be accomplished by putting the same time and resources into bettering man's condition.

One can only wonder in amazement why such beliefs continue in this era of enlightenment. The desire of man to live forever in peace and happiness explains some of the reasons for the perpetuation of the myth and superstition of eternal life. But one reason, and one reason alone, motivates people to continue their illogical, unproven beliefs in heaven and hell – FEAR. Without fear, religions would lose their most effective method of controlling the masses and religions would have little support, ultimately causing them to fade into history. When the fear of death is conquered, cathedrals will become museums and symbols of past myths and cultures.

The next question one must ask is how religions can continue to frighten the masses into believing dogma that cannot be proven. The answer to that is to continually indoctrinate people. Religions begin this process with young children even before they reach the age of reasoning. By constantly repeating that god, heaven, and hell exist, the members of the clergy indoctrinate new, young recruits.

The Roman Catholic Church became one of the wealthiest entities in the world by applying these scare tactics. Defrauding priests, bishops, cardinals, and popes have lived their lives in luxury while the gullible masses gave up their earthly possessions to support them. The masses were intent on getting the wonderful afterlife they were promised. Robert Ingersoll wrote, "If priests had not been fond of mutton, lambs never would have been sacrificed to God. Nothing was ever carried to the temple that the priests could not use, and it always happened that God wanted what its agents liked."

Although many religions and gods do not agree with one another, they band together to prevent the godless from having any say in the matter. They all work together to exclude nonbelievers from expressing their views by ridiculing and shunning them – even killing them. Daily we see the efforts of believers to force their beliefs on all others and prevent nonbelievers from presenting their comments and opinions. The insistence of "In God We Trust" on our money is a good example, even though no one leaves their welfare to a deity. The insistence of making everyone acknowledge god when pledging an allegiance to his or her country is another example. It should be obvious to all that if there is an all-powerful, all-knowing supernatural being, we are under its control just as we are under the control of the thug who has a loaded gun at our head.

Millions of dollars are spent placing Bibles wherever people congregate. Hotels, courthouses, and other public places are furnished Bibles without charge. Those buying these books for the public believe they are racking up brownie points from god, while getting a good tax deduction.

Religions use tradition, symbolism, rituals, and repetition to reinforce people's beliefs in their unbelievable dogma. The Christian symbol of torture and death, the cross, is placed everywhere – even around people's necks – presumably as protection against vampires. (Or are they trying to protect themselves from god?) The image of Jesus on the cross is a vivid and constant reminder of the power and cruelty of a god who created evil and threatens everyone with eternal damnation if they do not believe as he commands. How anyone can believe that god proves he is kind and loving by killing his only son is beyond comprehension. The first time god became angry with sinners he killed all of mankind except Noah and his family. The next time he is planning to kill everyone and send them to hell, except for the 144,000 Essene Jews who are to be saved. No Christians! Intelligent design, anyone?

If people would open their eyes and think logically, they would recognize that religion as practiced today is the biggest scam that has ever been foisted on the human race. We could ignore this fraud were it not for the bigotry, intolerance, and hatred caused by it. Religions must be put in their place if man is to survive on this planet. We can be sure that a religious fanatic would not hesitate to use an atomic bomb in the name of his god.

Lest you worry too much about an afterlife for which there is not one iota of proof, you can return to the contradictions in the Bible. While books by Pharisees promise an afterlife, books by Sadducees such as Job 14: 12, Psalms 49: 19, Proverbs 2: 18-19, and Ecclesiastes 9: 5 all say “When you’re dead, you’re dead.”

HEAVEN OR HELL

The Ultimate Sin according to Christians is not killing, not rape, not robbery, it is not believing in Jesus. What a deal! Every wrongdoing imaginable by man can be forgiven according to the psychotic, unemployed, wandering parasite, Paul. This salesman by nature, turned evangelist who never met Jesus, seemed to have a lot of insight into what god and his only begotten son wanted. Perhaps that blinding light penetrated his brain deeper than we thought. It was this character who obsessively traveled across the hot desert to spread the word of a new religion. The new rules that followed, which outlined membership requirements of this religion, were incredibly simple: believe in Jesus and you may commit any sin as long as you say "I'm sorry" before you die. It is frequently easier to ask for forgiveness than to ask for permission.

Only an idiot would not sign up and pay for a carte blanche ticket to eternal paradise. With this new religion, a person can steal, rob, rape, murder, and even covet his neighbor's wife without having to worry about divine punishment. This new and improved god of the New Testament, after years of killing millions of his children unmercifully, apparently decided to change the rules. Maybe god realized there would be more worshipers if they were allowed to commit a little sin while they were here on earth.

The current belief in Christianity is that any sin can be forgiven except the unpardonable one – not believing in Jesus. All a person has to do is to fill out the paperwork before he/she dies and get it notarized by the clergy. By following these simple procedures, a glorious eternity awaits. However, if one fails to make amends with his savior before the final hour, a different destination awaits. Don't forget to take a fan!

Theologians are now in a serious discussion as to whether unbaptized babies go to purgatory, limbo, heaven, or hell when they die. You would think that god would clear up that important confusion. The general consensus, based on biblical scripture, is that all children go to heaven if they have not reached the age of accountability, although no one can agree on what that age is. Retardation and other forms of mental impairment will get one a free ticket to the sky castle as well. Only responsible, sane, and mature folks have the burden of spending a lifetime trying to avoid hell. If you have not been told about Jesus, you are excluded from this club of the damned. No wonder the South Pacific islander natives got nervous when they saw a boat full of Bible toting white men approaching.

There has never been a published directory since Dante's *Inferno*, as to who is in heaven and who is in hell. One would think god would at least keep a record of all who made it to the celestial palace and all who did not. We would all like to think our dearly departed loved ones made the grade and squeezed through the Pearly Gates with approval. We also wonder about others in history who have moved on to the hereafter. Are all the popes in heaven? What about the cardinals, bishops, and pedophile priests? Did the adulterous preachers and ministers get to cash in on their divine insurance policies? Probably so, as they were special in god's eyes. After all, doing the talking for god, since he does not seem to want to do it himself, earns extra bonus points when it comes to reserving a room in the nursing home in the sky. If heaven and hell existed we would not have much trouble finding them. If hell existed, we should be able to find it with our heat detectors. Since a number of people have bodily risen to heaven, they should also be easy to find.

One can only guess that the guest list of the Abode of the Damned would be longer than that of the Happy Hunting Ground. The entry requirements for heavenly paradise are much more stringent. Anyone can get into hell. It is simple. For example, a devout believer who falls from the roof of a thirty story building might utter a few expletives on the way down, including using god's name in vain. That is a no-no and it will automatically cancel the eternal reservation and divert the poor soul into the dark, miserable abyss. Millions of folks die unexpectedly in this world and because of the suddenness, do not have time to make things right with Yahweh. It is understandable why a man being torn to shreds by a vicious shark attack does not pause long enough to ask for forgiveness of his sins, repent, and thank god for his love and mercy. One would think the poor fellow had more urgent matters at hand. Unfortunately, god does not bend the rules, not even for a man being eaten alive by a fish. No repentance, no heaven!

Other more fortunate people have plenty of time to get right with the lord. A convicted serial killer sentenced to execution usually has years to ensure salvation before the final needle in his arm. In fact, thanks to taxpayer dollars, priests and other clergy are made available to these wicked, perverted, despicable human beings so that they can make their future plans with Jesus. These murderers and rapists spend most of their time reading the Bible and asking for forgiveness, regardless of the number of innocent lives they brutally snuffed out. Remember, rape and murder are among the forgivable sins.

For those of you who are certain you are going to heaven, we would like to introduce some of your future roommates to you:

Dennis L Rader - Also known as the BTK (Bind, Torture, and Kill) killer, this lunatic brutally tortured and killed at least ten women from 1974 to 1991. A mostly unnoticed man, Rader was married with two children while he secretly led a debauched life of evil. He was a member of the Christ Lutheran Church for 30 years and president of the church board. After conviction, Rader expressed these thoughts, "I believe there is a god. You know, according to the Bible and Christianity, you can do terrible things and be accepted, but you can't keep doing it, you know."

Jeffery Dahmer - This psychotic nut committed acts of cannibalism, dismemberment, and necrophilia as he killed 16 young boys between 1978 and 1991. Just before he was beaten and killed in prison, he turned to Jesus and was baptized. According to the chaplain performing this ritual, "Jeff had nothing to gain in this life by being baptized; he had everything to gain in the next life. He was baptized for the same reason anyone else is baptized. He needed to be saved." That's for sure!

David Berkowitz - This New York City madman killed 6 young women in the late 1970s. He became famous as the Son of Sam. Upon incarceration, David found Jesus. Imagine that! He began Bible study groups in prison and even has a Christian website that he maintains behind bars. The website stresses that only Jesus can "change a serial killer and an avowed Satanist into a lover of people and a lover of god." He maintains that he was troubled as a youth. If he was troubled as a youth, imagine the damage he might have caused if his problems had been more severe! Regardless, he has made things right with the lord and has had his ticket to heaven endorsed.

Velma Barfield - A former Sunday school teacher, this Christian grandmother was executed in 1984 for committing four murders by poisoning, including two husbands and her mother. While in prison awaiting execution, Velma began leading Bible studies and counseling troubled women. The Rev. Billy Graham posthumously praised this she-devil. She once said, "I know the Lord will give me dying grace." Her prosecutor summed it up best by stating, "I probably brought more people to the Lord than Billy Graham. When they go to prison, they all find the Lord." Amen brother! If anyone becomes Velma's roommate in heaven, we recommend you don't accept her dinner invitation!

Adolf Hitler - Although we have written an entire chapter on this low-life madman, it cannot be emphasized enough the brutality he caused in the name of religion. Millions upon millions of innocent people were murdered because he was "Doing the Lord's work." Adolf was a devout Christian and if Paul was correct, should have qualified to pass through the Pearly Gates. Since god keeps no entrance records, we don't know for sure if all his evil sidekicks got to go with him. Maybe, at least Eva Braun squeezed through. After all, one needs sex in heaven, too.

God - No list of heaven's residents would be complete without mentioning the fact that the granddaddy of all serial killers not only lives there, he runs the joint! God single-handedly has murdered more humans on earth than all the others combined. Perhaps this is why he seems to have a soft spot for the despicable; they have something in common to talk about over dinner.

If we listed all the psycho-nuts who supposedly have made it to the Sky Castle, we would have to write several more books. Prudence would dictate that these inhumane killers would get no mercy for their heinous crimes. The laws of man seem to be the logical way to punish psychotic killers, but unfortunately according to myth, the laws of god override man's laws. We only thought that the U.S. Supreme Court was powerful. It does not hold a candle to the Hallowed Appeals Court of the Universe. This court overturns all earthly convictions simply by asking the condemned to say, "I'm sorry!" Logic and reasoning would make the inquisitive ask why even bother having a legal system in our society if god is going to override it. Perhaps there is truth to the bumper sticker that in emulation of the bishop who oversaw the massacre of Huguenots in 1572 said, "Kill them all, let God sort them out."

It is sad to think that so many evil people are enjoying the amenities of heaven while so many good people are suffering eternal damnation. This irrationality provokes one to ask, "What is god thinking? Or is he?"

For those of you who think you might not be qualified for the heavenly palace, we would like to introduce you to some of your neighbors.

Galileo Galilei - Astronomer
Mark Twain - Author
Charles Darwin - Naturalist
Robert Frost - Poet
John Adams - U.S. President
Alfred Hitchcock - Director
James Madison - U.S. President
Andrew Carnegie - Industrialist
Benjamin Franklin - U.S. Founding Father
Heller Keller -Lecturer
Abraham Lincoln - U.S. President
Gloria Steinem - Activist
Thomas Edison - Inventor
Bertrand Russell - Philosopher
Frank Lloyd Wright - Architect
Carl Sagan - Astronomer
Sigmund Freud - Psychoanalyst
Howard Hughes - Inventor
Albert Einstein - Physicist
Richard Burton - Actor
Ernest Hemingway - Author
Christopher Reeve - Actor

Isaac Asimov – Author
Thomas Paine - Founding Father
Stephen Jay Gould – Anthropologist
John Lennon - Musician
H.L. Mencken – Journalist
H.G. Wells – Author
Robert Heinlein – Author

These folks, like many others, have made wonderful contributions to enhance the world we live in. They have improved the quality of our lives by making advancements in art, literature, democracy, science, and theater. They will remain in people's hearts for generations to come because of the good they did for mankind. However, they all had one thing in common – they were nonbelievers and according to doctrine, they were sent straight to hell.

Since these folks were highly intelligent and educated, we must assume that if there are libraries, universities, and centers of intellectual thought in the afterlife, they must all be located in hell. Besides, the misfits in heaven would not use these facilities even if they were made available to them. If a person had to choose where to spend eternity, one would think that choice would come easily. As musician Billy Joel claimed in one of his songs, "I'd rather laugh with the sinners than cry with the saints…the sinners have much more fun!" When asked about his choice for eternity, a man once said, "I'll take hell; after all, that's where all my friends will be."

SPREADING THE WORD

One of the most harmful activities of religion is the insistence that believers should convince all others to believe as they do. Throughout history proselytizing, especially by the Christian and Muslim religions, has caused millions of deaths and untold misery. It is unimaginable to the authors how people can shun, harm, and even kill someone who does not accept an unproven belief. It is one thing to believe something that cannot be proved, it is quite another to insist that everyone else must believe as you do.

Two major religions, Christianity and Islam, expend tremendous sums of money to "spread the word." They send missionaries out into the world to perpetuate their beliefs. We see young, immature, clean-cut Mormon boys knocking on doors trying to preach to anyone who will listen to their version of an almighty god. One can only wonder as to how the world would be better if people spent the same amount of time working for humanity. To be fair, we must admit that many people working for god are socially conscious and work for the benefit of their fellow man. Just think how much more good could be accomplished if all the effort and money that Christians and Muslims spend on proselytizing were used for the betterment of society rather than building magnificent edifices and trying to convince all that their god is the one and only deity. As an afterthought believers will add, "If you don't believe in my god you will go to hell" or, "If you don't believe in my god, I don't want anything to do with you." It is this attitude that causes so much guilt and strife.

Family unity has been disrupted by teaching beliefs in the unknown and the supernatural to children before the age of reason. Imagine trying to convince children about a subject that mature, educated philosophers and scientists grapple with. Religious leaders have learned that to convince people of the ridiculousness of their beliefs, they must start early and force-feed those beliefs into young accepting minds. The clergy have also learned that if you inculcate a brain before the age of six and repeat it over and over, it becomes extremely difficult ever to shed that belief. Many will require psychotherapy and treatment to rid themselves of such beliefs when they realize they cannot be true.

The belief that humans have souls that live forever and are capable of feeling pain, suffering, and love, and that the soul can be saved from damnation only by believing a certain dogma or creed, causes tremendous strain in family relationships, especially when some members have reasoned that this belief cannot possibly be true. How can a parent or a spouse feel when their loved one does not live up to the guidelines of those who claim to know exactly how the soul is saved in the afterlife? One can readily see how families are torn apart by this belief.

Those religions that spread the word of love, tolerance, good health, and good human morality can be of value. Those religions that spread the word of intolerance, bigotry, and hatred are responsible for many of the conflicts in the world today. Those religions that threaten people with an eternity of suffering for not believing their dogma should create a nicer, more loving god.

As to the premise that people cannot be moral without the fear of god who will zap them after they die – that has been disproved long ago. The belief that god does not punish folks until after they die is so illogical that it defies comprehension. Few educated people actually believe this. God has become love in the minds of those who are kind, charitable, and loving. Tim LaHaye's books in the Rapture Series tell what Jesus is going to do when he comes back to earth. These books outsell those on logic 10 to 1. Millions really believe the terrible things their loving god is going to do to all who are not "saved." We cannot help but think of the many people who killed their loved ones because they loved them so much. Does humanity really need that kind of obsessive love? Can humanity even survive that kind of love? Like the dead spouse who was killed by her lover because he loved her so much, humanity may also be killed by "love".

Perhaps we need not be so pessimistic. We can readily see that educated, thinking people, though not necessarily disbelieving in god, have come to the conclusion that a god, if it existed, would be about love and goodwill. Thus we see people spreading the word that Jesus and god have been remade in the image of good, loving people. More and more people are disbelieving in Dante's hell and are creating a god and a religion of love. Society can only be improved by such a trend, though it will result in unemployment for thousands of dog-collared clergy.

Spreading the word means not only pursuing one's beliefs in religion and superstition, but requires all others to participate in their prayers, celebrate religious holidays, pray in school, acknowledge god on the money and in the pledge of allegiance, and accept statements of belief without question. Anyone who questions these beliefs or speaks out against them is required to remain silent under the threat of excommunication, even physical harm.

The Native American, Chief Pontiac, noted about the proselytizing missionaries, "They came with a Bible and their religion, stole our land, crushed our spirit...and now they tell us we should be thankful to the Lord for being saved."

One would think that a god who is all-powerful and all-knowing would be capable of spreading its own word. The JCM god is extremely jealous of other gods; he is not a good sport when it comes to a little competition. Like a child in a tantrum, he goes into a rage when he is not the center of attention. He burns cities and causes plagues to show his anger. He sends millions of people to hell because of their pagan beliefs. God needs to take some courses on anger management; they offer them at the local community college.

There is an old adage, "If you want something done right, do it yourself." God should practice this. For some reason he has relied on mortals to spread his word rather than spreading the word himself. Maybe he is shy and not a good public speaker. That is understandable.

God chose Moses as one of his earliest proselytizers. Moses went up and down the mountain numerous times to have discussions with god while his followers waited patiently at the bottom of the mountain to hear what the new rules would be.

God's pick of those to spread his word do not seem to be wise choices. We all make mistakes. But Paul? Pat Robertson? Paul was a pagan and delighted in the persecution of Christians. Pat Robertson could ace the admissions test to any state mental institution. An intelligent creator who relies on mortals to spread his word should be a little more selective when choosing designated representatives. Spreading the word of god should not be placed in the hands of imperfect mortals.

JCM believers are quick to point out that there have been thousands of other religions and ask, if they were true, why did they not survive? The answer is very clear – power. In some high school history books there usually is a chapter or two on the spread of Christianity. The single most common factor in the spread of religion is force. Force – psychological and physical – remains the main vehicle for the perpetuation of religions. Cortez and his merry band of thugs made a deal with the South American natives.

> We are going to steal, uh, I mean confiscate, your gold and send it back to Europe for governmental purposes, yeah, uh, that's right, governmental purposes. In return, however, we are going to do you a favor. We are going to destroy your ancient religion, one that you've had for thousands of years, and

> install a new, modern one. And when you finally begin to start believing in this new religion, we will release the thumbscrews and let you out of prison! On probation, of course.(Note: It's amazing how fast the Mayans and Aztecs found the Lord!)

Many societies and their religions have been completely obliterated by the spread of another religion. Imprisonment, torture, and execution have been effective tools in converting others to a new belief. Jesus' propagandist, John of Patmos, threatened the Nazirite commune in Ephesus, "So convert, or else I'll come to you soon and engage them in polemic with the sword that is my mouth." (Rev.2: 16 *The Compact Fully Translated Bible)*

Spreading the word – proselytizing – results in hatred and conflicts.

FEAR

Fear has a broad range of feelings starting with uneasiness and progressing to apprehension, anxiety, fright, dread, terror, panic, and finally a complete breakdown of one's ability to function. Phobia is a derivative of the Greek word phobos – fear. Phobia is an irrational, excessive fear of a particular thing or situation.

The fear of a supernatural being varies among people, from anxiety to terror. We have coined the term deiphobia for the irrational excessive fear of a god who cannot be felt, smelled, tasted, seen, or heard. No one has been able to prove that such a god exists; yet many are in constant fear of such a being.

Religions were originally created out of hope, fear, and ignorance. As the human brain developed, man began questioning the unknowns of the universe. The basic human questions of how, why, when, and where, did not generate easy answers. Humans are the only species in the animal kingdom capable of pondering their existence. We are also the only creatures on earth that are aware of our mortality. Such awareness has resulted in a fear of the unknown.

No emotion captivates and paralyzes mankind as much as fear. Fear can bring the strongest people to their knees. Fear can override reason, logic, and pragmatic thinking and has no intellectual barriers. However, man has developed an antidote for fear in the form of denial and superstition. The early religions of the world did not attempt to control their followers. Rather, they attempted to offer soothing explanations of the unknown and the frightening world around them. The fear of death and eternal nothingness was calmed by promises of an afterlife, which normally contained better conditions than the real life experienced on earth. Storms, diseases, and floods were considered the acts of angry gods. These angry gods could be appeased by sacrifice and worship, thus alleviating nature's calamities and reducing the fear and anxiety caused by nature's disasters. These beliefs are still prominent in many of today's religions, although sacrifice and worship have not proven successful in decreasing human suffering.

While many humans want comfort from their fears of the unknown, most accept their role in the universe as being devoid of meaning or purpose, except for the meaning they give to their own life. They can live long enriched lives without the need of divine intervention. Living a full life from birth to death, with nothing promised or guaranteed, is more than enough to make them happy and content. Who knows what happens after death? Life is lived on earth and not in some fictitious celestial paradise after death.

The fear of death is present in most people. The possibility that a person simply ceases to exist after death is incomprehensible to many. However, the fear of death makes no sense and has no purpose other than to place you under the control of the clergy. Religious leaders have used the fear of death to advance their agendas. By promising a wonderful afterlife or by threatening an eternity of suffering after death, religions have been able to control the masses. Afterlife has been a primary theme in many religions throughout the world. With the elimination of the fear of death, humans could go about their daily lives with purpose and meaning.

There is fine print in the belief of an afterlife. It requires one to dedicate his entire life to the priests or to the divine messengers who have direct contact with god. It is only the clergy who have a direct line to god. The clergy can relay instructions from god and let people know if god is satisfied or not with their performance. If god is not happy, people will have to mend their ways. Normally this includes more worship, more sacrifice, and larger contributions. It is easy to give up a little money for eternal bliss. These monetary contributions have allowed religious institutions to amass wealth and build magnificent edifices displaying fine art, all tax free.

It is important to realize that anxiety and apprehension, even fear, can be worthwhile and lifesaving, but phobias are destructive to the human condition. The anxiety that a woman has about walking alone on a dark street in a high crime area may very well keep her from being molested or assaulted. The fear of cancer of the lung may keep one from smoking. The fear of alcoholism may keep one from drinking excessively. There are good reasons to have fear, but the fear of the unknown that has not been proven is a different kettle of fish. The fear of failure, pain, punishment, disease, and death are prevalent in humans. Those fears may result in activities that prevent harmful effects and in that sense can be worthwhile. Severe dread and panic are always destructive. For example, a man running a large corporation, hiring, firing, and controlling many lives with confidence, may totally break down with fear when he flies in an airplane. He may promise the pilot all his wealth and fortune if he will only land the plane and get him to safety. Once safely on the ground, this individual regains his composure and conveniently forgets his promises. Intellectually, the man knows that he is safer flying in an airplane than riding in a car, but this knowledge does not overcome his fear of the unknown.

So it is with deiphobia, a fear of god. In some people this irrational fear controls their life. Although some believers have created a good god, many still have an intense fear of what that god has in store for them after death.

The believers have created a god who by their definition is perfect and knows everything that happens on the earth. At the same time, the believers see the prevalence of natural calamities, poverty, disease, and death on the earth. However, they are afraid to blame their god, the supernatural being that allegedly has the power to prevent such suffering. The believers then rationalize that this suffering must be man's fault.

Many religions control people with the fear of demons and evil spirits. These outcast characters are usually portrayed as having malevolent, supernatural powers and typically are associated with the sinners of the world. Religions have represented demons as dark and evil, waging war against light and goodness. People were considered demons when they had physical differences or deformities. In the New Testament people afflicted with leprosy or epilepsy were considered demons since man did not understand the causes of these ailments. Christian doctrine teaches that only Jesus was capable of purging these demonic intrusions out of the human body. Anxiety, depression, and other mental disorders were, and in some cases still are, considered the results of evil spirits. Fortunately medicine and science have a better understanding of mental and physical maladies today. Science has proven that the causes come from within the body, not from an external demon, god, or devil.

For those people who would not allow priests to control their lives, religion invented another method to convert the nonbelievers. This would become the granddaddy of all fear tactics. It was labeled eternal punishment. Eternal punishment quickly became the weapon of choice with Christianity. A new wave of fear could now be injected into the nonbelievers. This punishment came in the form of an eternal sentence to hell. The warden on duty was Satan. Satan represented all of the sins of the world and was considered to be the mastermind of evil. Although most religions have used the myth of a diabolical underworld as the final destination for the wicked, no religion has capitalized on hell as much as the JCM religions. No religion has used the punishment of hell more effectively than Christianity and Islam.

Fear can be used to force people into religion in two distinct ways. One is the fear of withholding the promise of a reward in heaven where everything is perfect and we reunite with our loved ones. If this does not work, religious leaders bring out the big gun of fear – hell. While many can accept death (do we have a choice) and its accompanying nothingness, the prospect of sitting on hot burning coals for the next zillion years is not very comforting. In fact, it is downright terrifying.

The fear of death is based upon a fear of god. We should not fear nothingness because we experienced nothingness without difficulty before we were born. We must admit, however reluctantly, that there is the wish and hope that we will live forever. This same wish prompted the Egyptians to bury their dead with possessions, money, even servants, in hopes of having eternal comfort. That wish never materialized. After thousands of years people finally had to admit, "You can't take it with you."

Fear is a contagious disease. We get it from one another. We get it from our parents, our peers, and our preachers. Legitimate fears can be lifesaving. The irrational fears are destructive to the human personality. Deiphobia, like all phobias, should be treated. People with phobias may require medications and psychiatric care to relieve those fears.

Some of the clergy are very effective when it comes to instilling fear into their followers. The fear of god, once instilled, gives the clergy control over the person with deiphobia. Many people give their life savings, even their lives, to persuasive clergy. One should observe, however, how few times the clergy have risked their own lives for the same cause. Fear does get results! Scaring people does work. As rational human beings, it is important to realize that we must choose the fears that we can and cannot live with. Unfortunately, most people in American society believe and respond to the fears of a wrathful, vengeful god.

It has been said that god is loving, forgiving, and merciful. Notice however, that loving people create a loving god; cruel people create a cruel god. People create the kind of god they want and one that suits their needs. Loving people create a god of love to justify their belief in god. We can only wish them well as love is indeed important to human existence. Unfortunately, one must hunt and pick only certain statements in the scriptures to find a loving and caring JCM god. By no human standards of morality or logic can the biblical god be called a god of love.

While many testify and believe that the New Testament god is centered on love and replaces the judgmental Old Testament god, such is not the case. The Old Testament god only threatened people with death at the end of life and when that was deemed insufficient, he threatened to inflict atrocities on their descendents down to the fourth generation. The New Testament god not only threatens people with death, but also threatens them with an eternity of pain and suffering after death. That is a long time to suffer as a penalty for a few years of sin. Only an evil creature would do something that monstrous. Most humans are more merciful, forgiving, and loving than the JCM god.

Since the early days of Christianity and Islam, and to a lesser extent Judaism, it has been known that religion could be spread by force. Even today that concept exists as one is forced to recite "Under God" in a pledge of allegiance to our country and forced to read "In God We Trust" on our money. These subtle ways are not nearly as bad as Constantine's or Cortez's use of force, but nevertheless they are effective. Cortez and his accompanying priests forced Christianity upon all of South America, Latin America, and Mexico under the threat of punishment and execution, proving once again that the guy with the biggest gun will prevail with his religion.

Forcing children to pray in school and public places is another example of the use of fear to coerce a belief in the supernatural. A young child choosing not to participate in religious classroom ritual is automatically shunned by teachers and classmates. As one author (CG) well knows, a youngster proclaiming not to believe in divine, supernatural authority is not going to be picked as a candidate for the most popular student award. Additionally, such individuals will not be invited to participate in the school's Christmas or Easter festivities. Unfortunately, most children go along with whatever beliefs that are bestowed upon them by their parents, teachers, and peers. Many fears are prevalent at an early age: the fear of rejection, the fear of disapproval, the fear of being alone, the fear of being physically hurt, the fear of not being socially accepted – the list goes on and on. There is little wonder why a young child will believe anything he or she is told. Once fear is instilled in a youngster's mind, it is all but impossible to eradicate it.

Millions of people believe in religion only because of the fear and force it exerts. They were introduced to the devil and his evil ways long before they were taught to tie their shoes or ride a tricycle. The teaching of eternal punishment comes from parents who were taught the same thing when they were young. They too were threatened with eternal punishment if they dared deviate from the mainstream dogma. The fear and anxiety of believing in a supernatural god will remain for some time, but as the fear of god lessens, there will be more tolerance, understanding, and love in the human race. Zeus knows, we need it.

THE WORLD AS ONE

For thousands of years people lived in small groups isolated from other groups. Their entire world was confined to the area they could cover on foot, horseback, or canoe. Each group, whether large or small, had its own language, laws, and religious beliefs. Most were not aware of others in different parts of the world. In fact, when the Christian Bible was written several thousand years ago, the earth was considered to be flat and enclosed in a giant dome.

Jesus Christ, supposedly all-knowing, did not realize that the earth was round. If he did, he surely kept this tidbit of information to himself. One would think that in his brief years as a teacher he would have spent his precious time educating people about the realities of the world, rather than turning water into wine at a wedding feast.

With the advancements in technology, transportation, and communication, the world has shrunk. It took Magellan's crew three years to circle the globe. Today we have satellites completing the same circle in one hundred minutes. These same satellites can determine what brand of beer you are drinking on your back porch, and relay this information to any agency within nanoseconds. Air travel and relaxed policies on traveling abroad have allowed us to move freely about the globe. Fifty years ago, high school and college students made their annual pilgrimages to Myrtle Beach. If their parents were wealthy, they might go to Daytona Beach. Today, students conduct their partying at such exotic places as the Caribbean Islands and the Mediterranean. If our parents visited these faraway places, it was considered a once in a lifetime experience.

When discussing human problems and the earth's problems, one is frequently asked in a disapproving tone, "What are you, a one worlder?" As if that were the worst thing a person could be. One can only reply with another question, "How many worlds are there? Is there more than one earth?" You would think after seeing pictures of earth from space, more would see and understand that the earth is not as large as early man thought. With the advances in transportation and communication it should be obvious that the earth is no longer considered infinite and those artificial boundaries do not stop pollution, disease, or the migration of people. One needs to look no further than our own United States borders to realize the tremendous amount of migration that is occurring.

No longer can we consider health problems as being restricted to one country or region. Centuries ago, plagues were localized to certain isolated regions of civilization. Though plagues, such as the bubonic plague, may have destroyed much of the population of a particular culture, they did not proliferate worldwide. With the advent of trade, war, and exploration, infections cross great distances and affect many cultures. The Spanish explorers Columbus and Cortez were responsible for introducing smallpox, typhus, and yellow fever to the Caribbean and Mesoamerican regions. They took syphilis back to Europe.

Today we see new outbreaks of infections spreading worldwide in a very short period of time. AIDS, the most fearsome virus today, is a health problem associated with every continent on earth. It did not take a six-month sailing voyage to transmit it around the globe. It took only a six-hour airline flight. AIDS is truly a worldwide health problem and does not differentiate who it attacks – Christians, Muslims, Hindus, atheists, adults, and children. Some Christians actually believe this indiscriminate disease is the work of god on sinners, mainly homosexuals. They think their god is punishing sinners in much the same way as he did when he flooded the earth. This is one of the most preposterous claims ever made. It is absurd to deny proven medical knowledge in exchange for ignorant, human superstition. For AIDS and other health problems to be conquered, we must remove religion from the equation and allow humanity to come together as one world. If the world is to advance, we must unify and admit that all humans are one.

Language, culture, and religion prevent people from understanding one another and breed intolerance and conflicts. Differences in language and culture can be overcome, but the differences and conflicts in the various gods seem insurmountable. Most people believe that all gods except their own god are false. The believer in one god and the nontheist with no god are only one god apart. For the human race to continue to survive, it must be understood that all humans are essentially the same. We must understand that whoever or whatever created us, it created each and every one of us with the same feelings, needs, and emotions. Unfortunately, breaking down religious barriers and admitting this will not be an easy task.

Early man had physical characteristics such as skin color, body hair, and physical agility that were region specific to meet the needs of man in his environment. As with all animals, these physical characteristics protected them from natural elements and predators, as well as allowing adaptation to the local climate. If man had not developed those adaptations to his environment, man like many other species, would have become extinct. The cause of this natural phenomenon is evolution and adaptation,

Over the centuries religion has been involved with racial differences and intolerance. Christopher Columbus, known for discovering the New World, is less well known for the atrocities he committed on the indigenous people of Hispaniola. Due to the differences in religion, culture, and physical traits, Columbus grossly mistreated them by enslavement and execution. The natives were hung in groups of thirteen "in memory of our Redeemer and his apostles." History shows countless other examples of European Christians persecuting different cultures because of their race and differences of religion. Spain's other infamous Christian conqueror, Cortez and the priests who accompanied him, attacked another race of humans, the South American natives. We all know the atrocities experienced by the North American natives.

The physical traits that determine the human race are rapidly diminishing. With the modern comforts of air conditioning and other residential amenities, people in hot climates will no longer need dark skin. Inhabitants of colder climates will no longer need body hair to keep them warm. People who previously required physical agility to avoid predators will no longer need this skill. It is obvious that whether you believe in Darwin's evolutionary theory or not, mankind is evolving towards one race.

The evolvement of mankind towards one race is being helped along by another phenomenon, interracial breeding. Marriage and procreation have been controlled by physical, cultural, and religious boundaries for centuries. Breakdowns in all three have allowed humans to begin interbreeding. It is becoming more common and more accepted for parents with different physical characteristics to marry and procreate. The resulting offspring are generating new physical and emotional characteristics that have never been seen before. As we advance into the twenty-first century, humans are going to become physically more similar to one another. At some point in the future, humans may physically become the same. There will be only one race of humans and society will be able to eliminate racism from our vocabulary.

As humans gradually evolve to become physically one, another yet larger obstacle must be overcome – religious differences and intolerance. This will be a challenge for years to come. Even as we realize we are the same, differences in religious beliefs will continue to keep us divided. For example, militant Islamic extremists are growing in numbers rather than diminishing. Catholic and Protestant feuds do not appear to be declining. Jews are still hated worldwide. Newer religions such as the Church of Scientology, Mormonism, Jehovah's Witness, Christian Science, and the Unification Church are emerging and are causing even more dissent among people.

As we become one race, it will be necessary to put aside myth and superstition. A practical approach would be to accept scientific knowledge as the basis of our civilization. If it is known to be untrue, it should not be taught. If it is not supported by a preponderance of the evidence, it should not be in our textbooks. Society should govern and conduct its affairs based on prudent, scientific knowledge. Unity and world peace will only be accomplished by abolishing ancient folklore and replacing it with modern scientific thought and realism. We may never have enough political power to abolish superstition, but we can educate and persuade. It is a long term effort. After all, Christianity has been around for over 2,000 years.

There has been a slow but definite trend towards merging governments. With advanced technology, communications, and travel, it is now possible to combine smaller governments into larger ones. Many United States cities and counties have merged to streamline the operation of government. No longer is it necessary for each small municipality in a county to have its own mayor, police chief, and building inspectors. Redundancy and costs are being reduced, saving tax dollars. Many states in the United States are adopting laws identical to other states. Doctors, lawyers, contractors, and other regulated professionals are abiding by a uniform set of standards as they cross state boundaries.

The establishment of the European Union consisting of twenty-five nations has made a significant advancement in world unification. Though each country has remained separate, the Union has enhanced political, economic, and social cooperation. Many functions have been integrated into one. Europe, like most of the world, is becoming smaller. Previously as each border was crossed, one encountered a different currency, language, and visa requirements. Travel between countries was extremely difficult and confusing. With the new European Union, established in 1992, there has been a consolidation of foreign affairs, customs, currency, health, and free trade. There is no doubt that this concept of integrating different societies will serve as a role model for other nations worldwide.

As world unity evolves, participation in organizations such as the United Nations will become more important. Governments will have to come together and establish policies concerning global conflicts, human rights, health, and religion. Abolishment of dictatorships is a must, but the means and methods of such abolishment should come from policies established by the majority of nations. A unified world will not allow a leader to go it alone.

Humans will continue to fight over property and power, with or without religion, but restricting religions to churches, synagogues, mosques, and temples is absolutely essential to good governing. There is no democratic society in the world under the control of a religious sect. The freedoms that our forefathers fought and died for should not be sacrificed to the fears, hopes, and ignorance of religion. We must now strive for freedom from religion if there is ever to be world peace.

Will there ever be one truly unified world government? Not in our lifetime. However, if a civilization of humans looks the same, speaks the same language, has the same needs, goals, and beliefs, there could possibly be a more peaceful, unified world. No society has ever failed because man was too reasonable.

A WORLD WITHOUT GOD

Whenever people criticize god and religion, they are asked in an exasperated tone, “What would the world be like without religion?” Or, “What would people be like without God telling them what is right and what is wrong?” Or, “How can people have any meaning in life without God’s instructions?” These questions imply that people would be cruel, immoral, and inhumane without god and that there is no meaning in life without religion and god. Religious believers imply this even though their own god is cruel, immoral, and inhumane.

By looking at Russia and China we can get a glimpse of what the world would be like without religion. While the governments of those countries differ from ours and deny some of the freedoms that we in democracies enjoy, their people are no more immoral for the lack of religion than those of other countries. In fact, Russia under a government that now allows religion has seen crime significantly increase. A god that makes one suffer after one dies rather than suffering immediately for one’s sins, is not an effective method for establishing human morality.

We can get a similar glimpse by looking at inmates in prisons. Overt nontheists constitute sixteen percent of the general population but only two percent of the prison population. Why? Because atheists recognize that they will be judged by human standards and cannot annul all offenses by promising god that they will not do it again. Al Capone's weekly reassurance from his priest that last week's murders had been forgiven and would not keep him out of heaven was the strongest possible incentive for repeat atrocities.

The belief that religion will give one meaning in life can easily be seen as the myth that it is. People create their own meaning in life and sad to say, many never have an opportunity to get beyond survival and procreation. The daily struggle for survival is the only option that many people have in their lives. Survival is a fulltime job for many people in the world. Ask a starving child in Africa about his meaning in life; undoubtedly the response would be food and shelter. If god gives worthwhile meaning to people's lives, it is doing a lousy job for that starving child.

Why is it so important that we have meaning in our lives? Is it really necessary to have meaning in life to enjoy a beautiful sunset, a good marriage, or fine food? The desire for a meaningful life stems from our parents' teachings. We are taught at an early age that life is worthless without meaning. We are brainwashed into believing that the only reason we are here is because god has a plan for us. This all-knowing god has actually taken the time to draw out a detailed plan for each and every one of the over six billion people that he has created on earth – all without the help of a legal staff. While this loving god has plans that some of us become renowned neurosurgeons and enjoy the good things of life, he also has plans that many are to spend their lives suffering from hunger, malnutrition, and poverty. He apparently has plans for millions of helpless children to die of cancer before they can even begin to think of a meaning for life. One can only wonder in amazement how god decides who gets what plan.

Without god, there is no anxiety about being zapped every time you make a wrong move. You are free to spend your Sundays as well as the other allegedly holy days doing what you please – not what someone thinks an angry, hateful, vindictive god wants you to do. If people help a person in need, they should do it for the joy and satisfaction of helping another human in distress, not to secure a front row seat in heaven. One can be in awe of the world without having to attribute its awesomeness to an imaginary, make-believe creator. One must realize that the meaning in life is what one does with it while here on earth.

It should be stressed that if there is ever to be a moral society, man must create it and enforce it. Many of the commandments of god are immoral by human standards. Believers justify god's immorality by maintaining that humans are just too dumb to understand god in all of its power, wisdom, and mystery. That is just another excuse to try to explain god's actions, which in reality cannot be explained or justified. Sigmund Freud wrote, "When a man is freed of religion, he has a better chance to live a normal and wholesome life."

So what would a world be without god? No devil to blame; no god to take credit for your good deeds; no fear of death or of what may follow death. Just think, life would end in nothingness, free of all suffering and pain. As Mark Twain answered when asked if he feared death, "I was dead for billions and billions of years before I was born, and had not suffered the slightest inconvenience from it."

A world without god would mean we could spend more quality time with our friends and family instead of wasting our time worshiping a make-believe character. Instead of planning for an eternal afterlife, we would be free to take our rewards while we could enjoy them.

A world without god would eliminate many wars. Without Allah, jetliners would not be slamming into buildings. A world without god would allow more spending on the needy, the sick, and the hungry rather than trying to placate god. A world without god would allow us to love each other regardless of race, national origin, sexual preference, or religion. Science would have free rein to explore new techniques in controlling overpopulation and eliminating human suffering. Without god, there would be more money to explore our solar system and our galaxy. We might eventually uncover the truth about the origin of the universe. A world without god would allow us to experiment with new medical advances so that mankind might have a longer, healthier, and more fulfilling life. Instead of giving our hard-earned money to religious fanatics such as Pat Robertson and the late Jerry Falwell, we could give it to St. Jude Children's Hospital to fund research for children.

A recent report published by the Church of England stated that contrary to its own propaganda young people are not on a "spiritual journey" nor do they have a "God-shaped hole" that they are longing to fill. In fact, young people are perfectly happy without a god and prefer other activities to fill their

Sundays. This research reveals that young people are happy with life and have no need for a transcendental something else, and regard the Church as boring and irrelevant. The number of young people going to church has halved since 1979. The number of children in Sunday school is less than a tenth of those in 1930. These studies scare the church folks who make a living preaching and instilling fear into their followers.

The British religion think tank *Theos* found that 43 percent of their respondents said that religion was not a force for good in society. Thirty-nine percent said that Christianity does not have an important role to play in public life.

The authors are convinced that a world without false hope and without the fear of god would be a great improvement over the delusional belief that there is a good guy in the sky looking after man's welfare. No doubt man will continue to use brute force and weapons of destruction to get his way, but at least without religion man would be responsible only to his fellow man. No more gods to take credit, no more gods to blame. It will be man, and only man, against natural forces.

John Adams wrote to Thomas Jefferson in his later years, "This would be the best of all possible worlds if there were no religion in it." H.L. Mencken wrote, "I believe that religion, generally speaking, has been a curse to mankind…that its modest and greatly overestimated services on the ethical side have been more than overcome by the damage it has done to clear and honest thinking. I believe that no discovery of fact, however trivial, can be wholly useless to the race, and that no trumpeting of falsehood, however virtuous in intent, can be anything but vicious…"

Commentator Andy Rooney wrote in his book *Sincerely Andy Rooney*,

> We all ought to understand we're on our own. Believing in Santa Claus doesn't do kids any harm for a few years but it isn't smart for them to continue waiting all of their lives for him to come down the chimney with something wonderful. Santa Claus and god are cousins. Christians talk as though goodness was their idea but good behavior doesn't have any religious origin. Our prisons are filled with the devout. I'd be more willing to accept religion, even if I didn't believe it, if I thought it made people nicer to each other but I don't think it does.

Frequently one reads and hears that man has a yearning for god. That yearning is used to explain a belief in god. In reality, people are inquisitive and have a yearning for truth; people have yearnings for health and safety; they have a yearning for comfort and life; they have a yearning to live forever; they have a yearning for someone or some being to give them hope and fulfill their wishes. Thus, humans created a supernatural, all-knowing, all-powerful being they call god. God is a wish.

We do not need to speculate what the world would be like without a god – we already have such a world. People just do not realize it. They continue to create gods that cause intolerance, bigotry, anxiety, and fear.

JUDAISM – ISLAM

Because we are writing primarily for nonbelievers and Christians, our main comments are about the gods of the Christian sects. However, the gods of Judaism and the gods of the Muslim faith have as much baggage as the Christian gods.

Judaism, because it is smaller, is a lesser threat to world peace than is Christianity or Islam. While Judaism has plenty of inane beliefs and traditions, those beliefs are far less harmful than the other two arms of the JCM god. Jews are a small minority in the world and as such have less influence as a religion. In addition, the Jewish faith has no absolute, dogmatic beliefs regarding afterlife and the Jews have not been instructed by their god to go out into the world and proselytize. Thus, they are not considered a threat to other religious groups. Jews are not "in your face" with the belief that their god is going to send everyone to hell if people do not accept their dogma.

Let there be no doubt about Islam. Islam is the fastest growing religion in the world. It is a threat to all who are non-Muslim and to many who are Muslim but belong to differing sects. The Muslims are now in the same position the Christians were in the Dark Ages, seeking out and killing those who do not worship their god. Religions appeal to uneducated economically deprived people. When religion is combined with unemployed young males who have few opportunities to make decent fulfilling livings, an explosive mixture is created. Since there is little hope for a decent life on earth, they rely on religion's promises for a blissful afterlife. For those devout Muslim believers, the process of achieving an eternity in heaven is accelerated by committing atrocities against infidels.

For a full understanding of the roots of Islamic violence, we must look back in history. Islam evolved hundreds of years after Christianity. This new budding religion grew rapidly in an area that was once predominantly polytheistic or pagan and it created a threat to the spread of Christianity. The response to this threat was the Holy Crusades and Muslims were savagely attacked. This competition between the religions was the impetus for the hatred between the Christians and the Muslims.

Today Islam is a threat to peace. While Christian morality has evolved beyond killing heretics, much of Islam, under the control of fundamentalist Muslim leadership continues to use brute force to make people believe their dogma. Even moderate Muslims are threatened with death if they express any doubts or questions concerning the religious tenets of their belief.

While we have discussed in some detail the problems with Christianity, we hoped that all would see the problems of Judaism and Islam as well. While it is true that we judge people by their actions, we must also take cognizance of their words. The bibles of religions are filled with intolerance, prejudice, killing, rape, and immoral behavior. While there are some moral truths in the bibles, it would be better to discard them all and start anew with bibles that teach love, morality, kindness, charity, and hope for humanity. The present bibles should be discarded – they are beyond editing.

Briefly let us look at some of the teachings of the Muslim leaders who have the power to compel people to act as they dictate. The Qur'an says about nonbelievers of their faith – infidels:

- It is the same whether or not you forewarn them, they will have no faith. (2: 6)
- Allah's curse be upon the infidels. (2: 89)
- We shall let them live awhile, and then shall drag them to the scourge of the Fire. Evil shall be their fate. (2: 126)
- But the infidels who die unbelievers shall incur the curse of Allah, the angels, and all men. (2: 162)
- He that denies Allah's revelations shall know that swift is Allah's reckoning. (3: 19)
- Those who reject our signs, we shall soon cast into the Fire: as often as their skins are roasted through, We shall change them for fresh skins, that they may taste the penalty: For Allah is Exalted in Power, Wise. (4: 56)
- Believers, make war on the infidels who dwell around you. Deal firmly with them. Know that Allah is with the righteous. (9: 123)
- Fight and slay the Pagans wherever ye find them, and seize them, beleaguer them, and lie in wait for them. (9: 5)

- Prophet, make war on the unbelievers and the hypocrites and deal rigorously with them. Hell shall be their home; an evil fate. (9: 73)

You find the same commandments in the Christian Bible; if you do not believe in my god you are going to hell where you will suffer an eternity of pain. The bibles give hope for salvation, but only if people believe in their prophets and their gods. Muslims, like fundamentalist Christians, believe their bibles are the literal word of god.

Religions are thus a threat to humanity. When religions preach love, kindness, and good health habits they may be of some value. When they emphasize the cruelties of an omniscient, omnipotent, perfect, supernatural being, they become a threat to man and earth.

NONBELIEVERS ARE ANGRY

Nonbelievers, when they express doubt in god, are frequently asked, "Why are you so angry with God?" Believers are perfectly content to tell all who will listen that their god is perfect and loving and if you don't worship their god you will go to hell. Of course they are not angry with you. They love you very much and are begging god (that is called prayer) to make you see the light so that you will not have to spend an eternity in god's hell.

But, if anyone expresses any doubt about a supernatural being, lo and behold comes forth, "Why are you so angry with God? You must have had a very disappointing and unhappy life. Why do you have no hope or meaning in your life?" It should be obvious that people who do not believe in god are not angry with god. Few people get angry at something that does not exist. The anger stems from witnessing the tremendous amount of suffering, torture, and killing that has resulted from a belief in god.

Yes, nonbelievers are frustrated and angry with the concept of a god that people insist exists. If their god is all-knowing and all-powerful, nonbelievers are angry that this god does not live up to basic human moral standards. God should be asked, with all of his power, why he does not do a better job running the universe.

Why god:

- did you create men and women to be sinful and cruel, then blame them because they are that way? (An all-knowing god would have known that Eve would be tempted to go against his wishes. She was created that way.)
- did you do such a lousy job creating the earth and the universe with all sorts of natural disasters?
- did you create a perfect ideal world for mankind in the Garden of Eden and then take it away?
- did you create evil? If the lower animals in the kingdom cannot sin, you should have stopped then with your creation efforts. You need not have fooled around with humans who do sin. (Man is getting powerful enough to destroy the human race, so we may not have to wait on you and Jesus to kill us all when you decide to separate the believers from the nonbelievers. You can be sure that whatever killing is done before that time will be done in your name.)
- did you, with all of your power and knowledge, allow your favorite folks, the Jews, to be persecuted and abused as they have been?
- do you sit idly by as children drown, starve, and develop diseases that you could prevent and cure in a second? (We thought you loved children.)
- did you create Saint Lucifer and then, when he didn't turn out well, let him loose to wreak

havoc on all humankind who are so weak that they cannot stand up to the evil force that you created?

- did you think that torturing and killing your son would prove to the world how merciful, loving, and forgiving you are?

As one ponders these questions and observations, one must come to the conclusion that such a god cannot exist. The alternative is that god is a monster. The most humane thing that one can believe about god is that it does not exist. To believe that such a god actually exists and still worship it is much more of a sin than simply not believing it in the first place. There is nothing in intelligent human reasoning that allows for worshiping an evil, supernatural monster.

Nonbelievers in gods, devils, angels, witches, fairies, saints, and demons are not dumb enough to be angry at something or someone that does not exist. They *are* angry and frustrated with people who have created gods who are omnipotent and omniscient, yet sit idly by as humanity suffers. They *will* continue to criticize such a being, even if it is nonexistent, as much harm has been done and continues to be done in its name. As we become a more humane and civilized society, we must ensure that future generations do not continue to cause abuses and atrocities to mankind based on belief in the supernatural.

Religious people are easily offended when logic is poked at their beliefs. They are comfortable telling others that they are going to hell if they don't believe as they do, but they have no tolerance for those who criticize their religion or their god. Most nonbelievers of gods and religions are open-minded to any possible proof or evidence of a supernatural being. The devoutly pious completely close their minds to any discussion that challenges their beliefs; even to the point of brainwashing themselves that the Bible's fourteen unambiguous endorsements of a flat earth do not really mean what they clearly say.

Nonbelievers *are* angry because they see the tremendous amount of sectarian violence occurring around the world. They observe hundreds of millions of people spending their efforts and resources attempting to pacify an imaginary monster in the sky, rather than trying to improve the conditions of humanity. Nonbelievers *are* frustrated when they see the failure of religionists to use logic and reasoning. Reasonable and logical people understand that an airplane may crash due to weather, mechanical failure, or pilot error, and it is not the result of god's will. They then strive to improve airline safety with better aircraft design and crew training; the religionists think that praying to god is the solution. Nonbelievers *are* angry when they witness a young child dying of cancer without medical treatment because the parents put all their faith in the hallowed healer, instead of in advanced medical technology. Yes, nonbelievers *are* angry, but not at god. They are angry and frustrated with their fellow human beings for allowing a make-believe deity not only to control their lives, but also to wreak havoc on humanity. Nonbelievers may respect, even love people with illusions, delusions, and silly ideas but they *are* angry when they are not allowed to criticize illogical ideas because everyone must respect religious dogma, no matter how ridiculous the dogma.

So god, when you come up to human moral standards and prove your power, knowledge and goodness, we will respect and worship you. Until that time comes, you will be judged by your actions and your non-actions. If you choose to ignore humanity and choose not to be a Good Samaritan, more and more people will ignore you and learn how to live good meaningful lives without the benefit of you and religion.

As we look at humanity, the earth, the planets, and the wasps that lay their eggs in the abdomen of a living spider so that when they hatch they can eat the paralyzed host from the inside out and as we observe the big animals eating the little animals, the kindest thing that can be said about god is that it does not exist.

THE IMPORTANCE OF FAITH

Faith is a belief in something that cannot be proven. With that definition we are all people of faith as there are many things that we believe that cannot be proven at this time. There are degrees of certainty of proof for all issues. No one can prove anything about the future, but there are degrees of proof based upon our experiences and knowledge that makes us believe strongly that tomorrow will come. On the other hand, a person with a terminal illness does not have as strong a belief that tomorrow will come. Even the healthy person realizes that a sudden, unexpected event such as a heart attack or an accident could immediately snuff out his life. Thus, even the belief that tomorrow will come is not absolute.

In this chapter we discuss faith in its more limited definition as used by most people. When people talk about faith they are using the word to mean a belief in the supernatural, god. While the dictionary's first definition of faith is unquestioning belief that does not require proof or evidence, the second definition is unquestioning belief in god and religious tenets. Although we shall discuss only the second definition, the unquestioning belief in god and religious tenets, we must admire Mark Twain's take on the subject, "Faith is believing something you know ain't true."

What is so admirable about believing something that cannot be proven? Does it make life easier? Does it cause one to make better decisions? Does it give happiness? Does it relieve anxiety and fear? If it does none of these things, then faith is of no value. If faith made people happier, kinder, more charitable, or more concerned about the future, then it would be of value even if it were not true. The problem with unquestioning, unproven, beliefs in gods, religious tenets, superstitions, and myths is that while some of these beliefs may give some people peace of mind, the overall effect is usually intolerance and bigotry. Heroin and cocaine can also give a person peace of mind but that does not justify their usage.

The faith that there is a good god, that there is a soul separate from the living body, and that there is a conscious life after death appears to give many folks peace and comfort. But does it?

If there were clear guidelines for obtaining everlasting happiness, free of pain and suffering, then such a belief would be a boon to humankind even if it were not true. One set of moral rules, acceptable by all, would be a boon to humanity. Think what a world would be like with one set of moral codes that all could agree upon. Alas, that is not happening and probably never will. As long as faiths are in such conflict we must keep those unproven beliefs out of our governing institutions. We have only to observe in history what has happened when one person's faith, or a group of people's faiths, gains control.

It is interesting to note that while people tenaciously cling to their unproven beliefs, they also insist that all others accept them. One reason is purely psychological. If a person can get another to believe as he does, he reinforces his own beliefs and that is comforting to the ego. Another reason is that happiness and peace of mind can result from the absolute belief that you are going to live forever, surrounded by your loved ones in a heaven so wonderful that it cannot be described. But LSD, heroin, cocaine, morphine, and Prosac can accomplish the same thing.

A third reason that people cling to their beliefs in a supernatural god is that they have been told over and over in a dogmatic, authoritative manner that such a being exists. Uneducated, inexperienced minds are forced to accept such repeated brainwashing without question. They eventually reach a point where they are no longer capable of thinking for themselves. These beliefs become ingrained in their brains, not to be touched by reality.

Probably the most important reason people cling to the belief in god is fear. Throughout history the various gods have been capable of causing hardship, illness, and suffering. Many gods are believed to pursue people after death and cause eternal pain and suffering. The fear of the supernatural keeps people believing. This fear allows the clergy to have their way with the unsuspecting. Without a fear of god, few people would be in church. Without fear of everlasting pain and suffering, cathedrals would become museums and relics of a past age. People are still afraid to eat from the tree of knowledge. As David Hume has written, "Men dare not avow, even to their own hearts, the doubts which they entertain on such subjects. They make a merit of implicit faith, and disguise to themselves their real infidelity, by the strongest assertions and the most positive bigotry."

At a recent meeting of the American Ethical Union, a speaker bemoaned the fact that it was difficult to get more attendance at the union's meetings. He wondered why the churches were filled while the attendance at the Ethical Society was so sparse. It was pointed out that the American Ethical Union, a most worthwhile organization, does not have the fear of everlasting damnation that religions have. There is the fear of jail, peer pressure, as well as a guilty conscience, but nothing surpasses the fear of an everlasting hell to get people's attention and control their activities. Many are willing to face the wrath of their fellow citizens, but few believers are willing to face the wrath of god.

We can confidently say that without fear, the religions of the world would change drastically for the better. People would be required to accept responsibility for their own actions. Faith and fear are necessary for any religion to keep its members in the fold.

Religion is the only area in the human psyche that does not require verifiable data. The creators of religions realized long ago that there is no verifiable data that will ever prove that god exists. There is no basis for a belief in the supernatural. The clergy have said for thousands of years, "Trust me. Just have faith."

Faith is extremely important to religious followers today. According to the scriptures, the ancient god made many appearances to verify his existence. He talked to many. The phrase, "And God said" is frequently used in the Bible. Today however, god has decided to talk to only a few, even though the population of the earth has increased a thousand fold. God's spokesmen now seem to be Pat Robertson and George W. Bush, neither a candidate for the intellect of the year award. No wonder people must use faith to believe in god.

Faith is important because the witnesses for god and Jesus did not have a lot of credibility. The disciples of Jesus were mostly unemployed vagrants looking for a cult. The faith required to believe in a religion is the same faith required to believe in flying saucers and the witnesses to both are just as unreliable. As H.L. Mencken wrote in his book *Treatise on the Gods*, "Theologians are well aware, deep in their hearts, that faith alone is not sufficient to make even half-wits believe in their mumbo-jumbo."

Faith is the only thing left when events occur that exceed the capacity of the human mind to comprehend. When dubious characters are the only witnesses to unbelievable events, one must question them.

You may want to accept things on faith, in fact we must accept many things on faith, but one should not be proud of the fact that one believes in something that cannot be proven. Faith is essential to religion, but reason, logic, and experience are essential to humankind. Some say that one must believe something before it happens, but in reality something must happen before one believes it.

Faith blinds people to reality – thus, "blind faith." Those blinded to reality will continue to be a threat to humanity. Faith separates people; doubt unites them.

END OF LIFE

As far as we know, the human species is the only one of the animal kingdom which is aware that its existence will come to an end. We humans have the distinct advantage or disadvantage of knowing that we will die. For thousands of years this knowledge has been perplexing and frightening. Why would an intelligent being exist, aware of its own mortality, and then suddenly or slowly die? What is that all about? Whether we like it or not, death is a fact of life, and yes – it will happen.

The knowledge of human mortality has been used and abused by religions for generations. Religions have promised every imaginable afterlife reward, from peaceful heavens to golden castles in the sky. Not one of religion's promises has ever been proven to be true. There have been no medically documented accounts of a resurrection, nor have there been any authenticated claims of post-life paradise. If there is a continuation of life's journey beyond death, we are not aware of it. Either it does not exist, or if it does, it is not meant to be known while we are alive. So why should we worry about it?

Most religions have used death and what follows after death as tools for controlling the behavior of their followers. Many after-death myths include post-life judgment of the dearly departed. A person's performance on earth would be judged by a panel of outer world justices to determine if the person was qualified for entry into the land of the dead. In some cases, punishment was administered to those who were not so humble on earth. Many wicked individuals were sent to eternal prisons such as Hades, and in some religions a place called hell, simply because the person didn't believe as the clergy required. Religions have used afterlife punishment/reward to control people's behavior, morality, and pocketbooks.

Death masquerades behind many veils. It can show its ugly countenance to a newborn infant or it can wait one hundred years. Death may occur peacefully while one is asleep or it may choose the interstate highway for a family traveling to their summer vacation. Accidents, murder, and disease are all weapons for death. Some people know exactly when they are going to die, while others do not have a clue. An inmate on death row can quote the exact minute of his demise. The shopper at the local mall shot between the eyes by a sniper did not see it coming. Most people have historically let death choose the time, place, and method, regardless of the pain and suffering leading up to it. Many believe in the age-old adage, "When it's your time to go, it's your time to go." That is fatalism, not religion. Most humans do not know the time, place, and method of their departure from life. It is not a subject we tend to discuss. We would rather let death do the deciding.

Others, however, have such a strong grasp on their mortality that they want the right to decide the terms and conditions of their death. They would rather control their destiny rather than let their destiny control them. Suicide has been a human occurrence since the beginning of humankind. We are the only species capable of contemplating and carrying out self-inflicted death.

There are many reasons a person chooses to end his/her life. Some are easily understandable while others are not. A healthy, financially secure twenty-one-year old male may commit suicide over the break up of a romance. This is difficult to understand but is most likely the result of depression which could effectively be treated with medicine and counseling. A ninety-two year old man in a nursing home, suffering with a terminal illness and the recent loss of his wife of sixty years, is another matter. This individual is experiencing severe physical and emotional pain and realizes that his existence on earth is no longer worthwhile. He does not want to endure further pain and decides that it is best to terminate his life with dignity – under his terms and conditions. The many suicides in today's society disprove the myth that god does not give people more problems than they can handle.

Over the centuries many millions of people have suffered needlessly while dying with excruciating pain and no hope of recovery. Religion has interfered in these matters as well as in many other facets of human life. Most religions have maintained certain beliefs regarding the act of suicide. Many threaten an absence of afterlife or even eternal punishment for taking one's own life. Superstitions and supernatural fables once again control and override man's logic, even when suffering and pain is involved. On the other hand, some religions condone suicide under the terms and conditions of that particular religion. For example, suicide committed as an offering to god is acceptable. A healthy twenty-five-year-old Islamic extremist with explosives attached to his waist may blow himself and fifty others to pieces. This is perfectly acceptable and will get the individual a ringside seat alongside god. However, if a suffering terminally ill cancer patient decides to take an overdose of sleeping pills, lo and behold the consequences as the doors to heaven slam shut and the devil escorts the hapless sufferer straight to eternal hell for denying a sadistic god the pleasure it derived from savoring the agonies of the suffering. The chances are that this distraught patient worshiped and prayed to god during his entire lifetime, but when god refused to answer his prayers for relief, the patient relieved his own suffering. Because of that – hot coals and fire. What a terrible ending for a good decent person who only wanted a quality pain-free life.

For centuries humans have euthanized their pets and other domestic animals to alleviate their pain and suffering. While the animals have no choice in the matter, most people believe it is inhumane to keep their pets alive when they are in irreversible pain. The financial burden takes its toll, as well as adding more days and weeks to the suffering animal. Many humans have the same attitude regarding their own lives when confronted with a debilitating disease or injury that has no cure. Issues such as cost to family members, cost to society, and just the lack of a quality life, play an important role in determining whether a person wishes to stay alive.

While some folks have the ability and the means to communicate and even carry out their wishes, others do not. A comatose patient in a vegetative state may never be able to carry out life or death wishes, or to relay these wishes to others. The recent case in Florida involving Terri Schiavo is a good example. A fluke seizure left her on life support for many years. Doctors determined that she had no brain function and would never recover. Her husband stated that she would want termination of life support under such conditions, but every religious zealot and politician in the country stepped in to play god. An unprecedented Congressional session was held to determine if the government should intercede in this family's affairs. Several levels of the court system heard arguments from both sides on whether to keep her alive or allow her to die. Such life and death decisions should be made by family members and not by an overzealous, fundamentalist, theocratic government. It is hoped that the new generation of centralized computer medical records will enable people to document their desires if such events occur. Recording this information in a will and power of attorney is also prudent, as well as notifying next of kin.

Physician-assisted suicide is another controversial issue in the right-to-die debate. While many medically ill patients cannot come to terms with the concept of placing a loaded pistol in their mouth, they can accept a less violent ending to their suffering. Assisted suicide could be a viable option. A pre-arranged death whereby a patient merely goes to sleep and never awakens is taboo to the clergy and religious leaders. Dr. Jack Kevorkian, known for his bold and innovative willingness to assist suffering patients in ending their lives, was imprisoned by the government for his activities. Dr. Kevorkian is a modern day Galileo by bravely challenging the church on its ancient doctrines, even when he knew such challenges would ultimately cause his own persecution and prosecution. His incarceration is making him a martyr. Our world is evolving away from the dogmatic control of people's lives toward a more secular and logical ideology. Future generations will appreciate the efforts of Dr. Kevorkian for attempting to make people's deaths more humane.

Every person wants to die peacefully without pain. While advances in medicine have greatly enhanced this wish with pain relievers and sedatives, it still has many limitations. Many debilitating diseases such as cerebral palsy, multiple sclerosis, and certain cancers have no known treatments or cures. One may only speculate why a loving god would inflict one of his children with cerebral palsy, a condition with no known cure. This devastating disease, while crippling the nervous and muscular systems of its victim, is cruel enough to allow the inflicted patient to live a long, miserable, and suffering life.

> Hello, loving god! What is this all about? Were you having a bad day or is this just one of your practical jokes like the one you and the devil pulled on poor old Job? Oh, you have a plan for this poor soul? One must consider your plan rather sadistic. What's that? Oh, if he commits suicide to relieve the suffering you imposed upon him, you're going to send him to hell to continue

> his suffering for eternity? Since you destroyed his nervous system, how can you know if he believes in Jesus? Since he can't speak or communicate because of what you did to him, or at least allowed to be done to him, we will never know what he thinks. My guess is that he doesn't want to spend eternity with you in heaven. He probably realizes that the devil can't be nearly as brutal as you have been, Big Guy! Anyway, the rest of the family is gathered around the dinner table saying grace and thanking you for all the food you gave them. They're all overweight and overfed, but thanks for giving them more food. Oh, if you happen to think about it, Oh Lord, please send some of this meat loaf to Africa where you are allowing millions of children to die of starvation! Amen!

A recent Supreme Court decision ruled 6 to 3 that John Ashcroft, in his capacity as US Attorney General and acting as god's messenger, could not prosecute physicians acting legally within the guidelines of Oregon's assisted dying laws. The Federal Government, with a strong push from those who speak and listen to god, has done everything possible to prevent people from making their own personal end of life decisions. As time goes on, more and more will realize that man and man alone plays an intelligent role in his final living days on earth. We can be thankful when the Supreme Court finally rules in favor of what is best for man and not be influenced by their personal childhood beliefs as to what is best for god. If god has enacted laws, then god and his angels should enforce them.

Those who are against suicide should be told clearly and bluntly, "Then don't commit suicide, but keep out of my death." Perhaps we should add death to the rights of life, liberty, and the pursuit of happiness. Death is an immutable fact of life and society should allow as much freedom as possible as we carry out that final phase of life.

THEISM – NONTHEISM – REALISM

Theism is a belief in a supernatural being. Atheism is the belief that there is no supernatural being or as some atheists prefer, "Atheism is without a belief in supernatural beings." Realism is the belief that we must find truth and accept things as they are and that humanity can expect no help from a supernatural being.

Whether one is a theist or a nontheist does not seem to matter during one's lifetime. (Atheist and nontheist are used interchangeably in our writings.) The rain falls on the just and the unjust in equal amounts. As one looks at life, one observes that the believers in a deity have the same problems as the nonbelievers. If a supernatural being exists, it shows no favoritism to any of the religious sects that praise and worship it. God has shown no inclination to make life fair and there is no reason to believe that it will make an afterlife of fairness and happiness.

For all practical purposes, whether one is theistic or atheistic has no bearing on life. The animosity and conflict between believers as well as between believers and nonbelievers is counterproductive to human achievement and does nothing but waste time and cause harm. No one is hurt if one is a nonbeliever. No one is harmed if one is a believer in the supernatural until the believer finds it necessary to force his belief on others.

The only reason atheism exists is because theists claim there is a god. Had this claim never been made, there would be no atheists. We are witnessing the emergence of realism, which tends to ignore both groups. The ultimate mindset of all people will slowly change to realism as more people discard claims of a divine supernatural being and find that their pleas to the supernatural go unheeded. The results will be people who only believe in what can be seen, heard, felt, and experienced.

Is it possible to defuse the conflict and hatred between believers and nonbelievers? Probably not. Atheists do not hate theists; they just want them to stop hurting others in the name of their imaginary god. In an ideal world both would be able to set aside their differences and become rational, logical, reasonable realists.

The authors' writings are an attempt to expose some of the harmful effects of fanatical religionists. The theist should say to the atheist, "You don't believe in god and I do, so let's get on with our lives." Much could be achieved if both could agree to disagree in a peaceable manner. In such a situation both would become realists and face life as it must be faced.

Realism focuses on what exists, not on beliefs that cannot be proven. Realism is awareness of the many things that have not been proven. Rather than explaining the unknown with a supernatural power, realists look for natural causes. Realists are willing to admit their ignorance and strive to investigate and discover the answers to the mysteries of the universe and life. Realists welcome questions and truth as it evolves, even if it disturbs their previous beliefs. To explain a mystery with another mystery solves nothing. Fantasy is not an unwelcome human activity, but when it masquerades as reality all sorts of bad things can occur. Fantasy interpreted as reality is insanity.

Theists and nonatheists must shift their thinking to realism if there is to be any improvement in the human condition. The arguments of the existence or nonexistence of god only distract from finding solutions to human problems. Even believers admit that god works in mysterious ways and cannot be predicted or described.

Realists are willing to await proof of a supernatural existence. Until such a divine being proves its existence with deeds and events that cannot possibly be natural, realists will withhold judgment. Realists will live their lives based on truths, which can be evaluated, tested, and reproduced.

It would be great if we could say to one another, "You are a theist, I am a nontheist." Or, "You are a nontheist, I am a theist." Then admit, "We both must be realists to get along in this world."

Perhaps we should mention another theism – apatheism. "I don't know about god and I don't care." The authors would embrace apatheism if it were not for the harm done in the name of religion.

STEP OUT GINGERLY

Nonbelievers in the supernatural – atheists if you will – are the last minority to be allowed free expression without being crucified. Blacks have become free, homosexuals are almost there, but atheists remain quiet and subdued for the most part. The time is rapidly approaching for atheists to come out of the closet.

Many atheists must still remain quiet while loudmouthed, dogmatic religionists spew their hatred for all who do not believe as they do. As time goes on, more can step out gingerly and express their views. All can and should express their thoughts when religion is used to prevent advancements in civilization under the pretence that god does not approve. Man, not god, is responsible for man. God, at least an all-powerful one, is responsible for getting whatever he wants. When people tell you what god wants, they should be promptly told, "Tell god to do it himself. What is he, on vacation or just plain lazy?" It is about time to assume that if god exists, he's a big boy and can take care of his own needs and desires. He can fetch his own burnt offerings.

While many of the clergy use hatred, excommunication, and physical violence against atheists, there is still a large number of believers who are reasonable and logical and do not approve of the religious fundamentalists who refuse to open their minds to reason and logic. These reasonable, logical, kind people of religion must join with the deists and atheists to produce a kinder, less warlike society. As has been stated before, it matters not what you believe about a supernatural being, it does matter how you treat your fellow man and the environment. All reasonable people should unite to better the plight of the human race and the world we live in. Theists who spout off on god's desires should be informed that god can take care of itself and enforce its own laws.

Meanwhile, atheists must recognize that coming out of the closet in a society where most people believe in god, is still fraught with losing friends, jobs, even life. In most social situations one must bite one's tongue and remain quiet. Sixteen percent of Americans have the confidence and intestinal fortitude to admit to opinion pollsters that they are nontheists. But given the social and economic consequences of such an admission, the true figure is more likely twice that. The dangers of being an acknowledged atheist in a society permeated with the contagious insanity of religion was spelled out in graphic detail by H.G. Wells in *The Country of the Blind.* Nonetheless, time is on the side of science, truth, and logic.

It is impossible to imagine the turmoil of those like Bruno and Galileo who bravely stepped out and challenged the church's doctrines and superstitions at a time when nonbelievers were imprisoned, punished, and executed. No one will ever know how many innocent lives have been destroyed because they did not believe in gods and supernatural powers. How many careers have been shattered? How many marriages have been torn apart? How many business contracts have been lost because someone had the courage to say, "I don't believe in god."

Many preachers realize the absurdity and the ridiculousness of their sermons. An intelligent, inquisitive pastor cannot keep from thinking that what he is preaching is cruel and inhumane. Dan Barker, a former preacher, delivered his sermons for years before realizing that he could neither accept nor believe what he was preaching to his congregation. Dan decided to come out of the closet and went on to write *Losing Faith in Faith* and became co-president of the Freedom From Religion Foundation. He has become an outspoken advocate for atheism and separation of Church and State.

If there is one point the authors want to make in this book, it is that nonbelievers are not alone. Millions of normal decent people are living their lives with hidden sacrilegious thoughts. They are fearful and most think they are alone. But they are not. Doctors, lawyers, scientists, pilots, politicians, and everyday citizens constantly pass one another on the street, not realizing they think alike. They each have their own reasons for remaining quiet. The lawyer's boss opens his meetings with a prayer; the doctor's friends attend the Baptist Church; the pilot's wife has wealthy Christian parents who will only leave their money to the children who believe in Jesus; the politician knows most of his votes come from religious believers.

It is now time for more people to test the climate. Those who are making a living amongst the dogmatic, emotional, flat-earthers may want to put a foot out to test the climate. Those who have less to lose should step out boldly and completely and be in the forefront in the battle for equal rights. Deists and atheists will have to fight for their rights, just as blacks and other minorities have had to do. Those who have less to lose must take the lead, but all thinking people must step up when religionists throw out illogical, harmful comments.

Atheists will have their wins and losses. They must pick the time and place for their battles. On occasions, the younger coauthor (CG) has remained quiet while bigots spat out their beliefs. Similarly, the older coauthor (JAH) has frequently decided not to stir the pot. He maintains that this is based on wisdom, but it is just as likely to be based on fear. As a medical examiner for the county he is frequently called to testify in courts of law. As such, he is instructed to place his left hand on the bible, raise his right hand, and swear to tell the truth – so help him god. When that occasion first arose, he did so quietly without fanfare, but vowed he would do that no more. But lo and behold, he did the same thing the next time and the next. Wisdom? Fear?

As civilization progresses, we will come to realize that religion, witchcraft, sorcery, and superstition should not rule the earth and its inhabitants. We will also come to realize that morality and human behavior come from man and not from the supernatural. More people must come out of the closet and show pride in their nontheistic realism, even if gingerly at first. Hopefully, there will come a day when nontheists can hold their heads high without being subjected to the hatred and bigotry of believers of the unproven and the ridiculous.

In an interdependent society each of us must determine when and where to express our beliefs. This is true with religion, sex, politics, and how your spouse looks. We should not get too depressed if we make the wrong decision occasionally, unless of course it pertains to how your spouse looks. H.L. Mencken once remarked that we should respect the other fellow's religion, but only to the extent that we respect his belief that his wife is beautiful and his children smart.

Richard Dawkins has written, "Those of us who have for years politely concealed our contempt for the dangerous collective delusion of religion need to stand up and speak out. Things are different now. All is changed, changed utterly."

GOD'S WILL

If an all-powerful, all-knowing, supernatural being exists and desires something, it would, could, and should get it without benefit of help from man. Over and over we hear people not only declaring what god's will is, but feeling the necessity to help god get its will. The request in the Pater Noster (Lord's Prayer), "Thy will be done," or, "May your whims be gratified," begs god to do its will. Why should fallible, weak, finite man have to beg god to do its will? If a powerful supernatural being exists, it will do its will whenever and however it wants.

One must wonder about god's will. According to the JCM scriptures, the omnipotent god created the entire universe. Thanks to Galileo and other heretical astronomers, we now know the universe contains billions of galaxies. Each galaxy contains billions of stars and even more planets and moons. The distances between them are trillions of miles and stagger our imagination.

For some unexplained reason, god chose to spend all of his energy on the inhabitants of a tiny area of earth now known as the Middle East. In fact, the Bible's stories are entirely focused on this miniscule portion of the universe. While we know there were much older, more advanced, and more populated civilizations in the world at the time of Abraham, there is absolutely no mention of them in the Bible. Instead, god was preoccupied with the wars being waged between Israel and Egypt and between the tribes of Israel. God's will was to interfere with the lives of these people and totally ignore China, Japan, and all others in the world. He never made an appearance anywhere else. There is no mention of Abraham's god in the bibles of the Incas, Aztecs, Europeans, East Asians, or any of the Native American tribes. If god's will was to make its existence known to all of humankind, he did a lousy job. Perhaps god did not realize that there were other people in the world, an easy oversight even for god, especially since he was so busy trying to get a few Israelites to worship him and bring him burnt offerings.

God supposedly issued rules to humankind to achieve human morality and goodness. Instead of making an appearance to all the peoples of the world, he only talked to Moses on top of a mountain. Moses met god face to face. Anyone else who looked upon god was to be killed.

Followers of the JCM religions imply that since god was so busy running the affairs of the Israelites, he had no time left for the others. This is interesting because the same culture's Santa Claus can visit every dwelling in the world in one night, a feat god could not accomplish. God supposedly delegates some of its workload to missionaries to spread the word. God told these selfless servants to eradicate the thousands of other peaceful beliefs and tell the uninformed about Jesus. If these poor primitive pagans refused to believe, their conquerors were allowed to use guns for additional persuasion. As backup persuasion, they were reminded that since they had been told about

Jesus, they were now immediate candidates for hell and damnation if they did not accept the new faith.

> Eskimo: If I hadn't been told about Jesus, would I still go to hell when I die?
>
> Priest: Well, no, not if you hadn't been told.
>
> Eskimo: Then why did you tell me?

Civilizations got along just fine for thousands of years without any knowledge of Jesus and Muhammad. Furthermore, Abraham's god hasn't made much of an improvement on civilization since its conception.

If you want to see god's will first hand, go to any hospital. Go to a makeship temporary morgue and view the charred remains of 200 of god's people following an airplane accident. Go to the tsunami-ravaged area and see the corpses hanging from the trees. Take a trip to Africa to observe millions of AIDS-infected, starving children. That surely will convince you of god's will. If one refuses to question god's will, then one refuses to think.

We repeatedly hear the excuse that "god works in mysterious ways" to explain nature's disasters and the misfortunes in people's lives. The same people who do not understand why god allows hurricanes, tsunamis, and human suffering know exactly what god's will is regarding homosexuality, slavery, women's rights, abortion, sex, suicide, and stem cell research.

Bertrand Russell, the noted agnostic-atheist, was once asked if he would be willing to die for his beliefs. His reply was, "Of course not, I could be wrong." Those who think they know god's will should be humble enough to admit that they too could be wrong.

Instead of discussing social issues in an absolutist dogmatic manner by declaring what god wants we should sit in conference and decide as unemotionally as we can, what man wants and needs. We should not have to seek god's will. God can take care of its own wants. It is the duty of man to decide what man needs, what man wants, and what is best for humankind.

God's will is man's will projected into a make-believe god by people trying to control others. It always has been and always will be.

THE AGE OF ENLIGHTENMENT

At what point in one's life does one become aware of the impossibility of a personal god as described in the JCM religions? The majority of people who have been indoctrinated with a supernatural being never reach the point of disbelieving that their god is going to take care of them after they die. They recognize that he/she/it is not doing a good job of caring for them while they are alive, but come death, there will be heaven. Why this majority never comes to grips with logic and reality is easy to understand since they have been so frightened with a god who zaps people for eternity that they simply follow Pascal's wager. They tell themselves that if they believe and are wrong, so what? Just do not take a chance on disbelieving in a god who has created fiery furnaces to torture them for an eternity in a hell that can only be described in a sadist's dream.

On the other hand, like the authors, many are left at the starting gate. Early in their lives they found that logic and reason did not support the belief in an all-powerful, all-knowing, loving, supernatural being.

One of us (CG) grew up in poverty. His father developed multiple sclerosis when he and his twin brother were two years old. While many MS patients live long fulfilling lives, their father rapidly deteriorated in four years. There was nothing any physician could do but sit back and watch as this debilitating disease slowly destroyed his central nervous system. A horrible death followed, leaving a grieving widow and two six-year-old boys alone and frightened – with no money. As the mother cried and wailed over the dead body, the attending physician escorted the confused twins out into the hall of the apartment building. He calmly stated that Jesus had taken their dad to heaven and that everything was according to god's will. The young future author told the astonished doctor that he was full of shit and refused to accept such a weak explanation as to why such a travesty had occurred. To this young boy, there was no god in the universe who would do this to a young family. If god had stepped up to the plate like a man and taken care of this grieving, poverty-stricken family, the author might have reconsidered his beliefs. But after brutally killing his father, god left town – nowhere to be found. God did not provide severance pay or any other compensation. He did not provide food, which so many Christians thank him for at every meal. God ignored the prayers of a young widowed mother, suddenly thrust into the head of the household after seven years of caring for a dying husband. A deity who could create billions of galaxies and flood the entire world could not manage to spare a dime for the poor widow and her children. The young lad figured that either such a god was not worthy of adoration and worship or that such a god did not exist. He decided on the latter and has never found any evidence since that a supernatural being exists.

On the other hand, the senior author (JAH) was fortunate to have been born in a stable family that even in the depression was able to live comfortably though frugally. He was sent to church and Sunday school but he was not burdened by an insistence of his parents that he must accept the myth of Jesus or rot in hell. He was allowed to think and reason and allowed to come to his own conclusions. Initially after listening to the preacher threaten, rant, and rave, he decided to believe and not take a chance on not believing. He figured it was better to say that he accepted Jesus and go on with his life, as it did not seem to make any difference in people's lives whether they believed in Jesus or not. However, Pascal's logic did not last long as he realized that if god existed, it would be able to read his mind and would know what he really believed. So, at an early age he decided to believe what seemed to be logical and reasonable and hope that if a god existed, it would understand how he came to his conclusions and that it would be the kind, forgiving, loving god as many people claim.

There are a great number of people who, like the authors, have become realists, skeptics, and nontheists at an early age. Though they may not have felt free to express their thoughts aloud, they quietly maintained their religious skepticism throughout their lives.

There are others who become nonbelievers as they reach a time in their lives when they feel comfortable contemplating life and the world around them. If they happen to be kind and charitable, they ask themselves how any god could be like the JCM god. Although it may be painful and cause considerable guilt, they finally come to the conclusion that it is impossible to believe in such a god.

A large group of believers lose their beliefs as they become more educated and encouraged, even required to think critically. Many colleges and universities stimulate and require their students to think. In fact, many parents have become upset when their children come home from college expressing thoughts and opinions that their parents cannot abide. The children come home with a new understanding of philosophy, logic, and science. They cannot help but reason and think about such issues as life, death, and first causes, as well as how and why things happen. (So parents, if you want your children to be good Christians or Muslims, keep them out of college, or at least send them to a Bible college where they won't be allowed to think.)

There are those who study religion and the Bible and eventually become convinced that a god as depicted in the JCM religions could not possibly exist. Even fundamentalist evangelists have come to the realization that the concept of god is no longer reasonable and they can no longer preach that it is. A number of preachers have become atheists by reading the Bible and using their intellect. Others whose livelihoods depend on religion will simply create a Jesus or a god that is love and ignore other teachings of the Bible. They will do as the Anglican Church has done – erase the threat of hell from their doctrine. If you want to become a nontheist, read the Bible with your brain, not with your emotions, especially the emotion of fear. As the author Mark Twain once said, "It's not the parts of the Bible that I don't understand that bother me, it's the parts of it that I do understand." It has been reported that 44 percent of preachers do not believe in a god like the JCM god but they will continue to preach, as their livelihood depends upon it.

Finally, elderly women and men as well as the disabled may reach the point of doubt and enlightenment as sickness, disability, and death come to them with no help from god. At that point they can no longer believe in a personal caring god. Though they have been brainwashed that god does not give people more problems than they can handle, they finally realize that it has all been a big fraud. Depression, psychosis, and suicides prove that people *do* have more problems than they can cope with.

You may ask why people go to their deathbeds believing in unproven myths and beliefs of god and eternal life. There is no doubt in the minds of the authors that fear is the biggest factor. For those who believe in a god who not only let Saint Lucifer escape from heaven to become Satan, but also created a hell for all who did not live up to his expectations, that fear is overwhelming. Although god's desires are never well expressed by god, they have been dogmatically expressed by god's middlemen – the clergy. These divinely designated pushers maintain that they are special, that god personally handpicked them to spread his word. They insist they have a heavenly hotline to the creator and know exactly what it wants. The fear of god makes many, if not most, follow Pascal's wager. Hope for eternal life and being with loved ones after death is reason enough for believing the unbelievable, but this alone does not get people into church. Without the fear of god, churches would be empty.

While many people realize the foolishness of religion early in life, others come to this realization at a later time. The reasons for this enlightenment are many, but the underlying reason is that these folks finally get the courage to discard their fears and take off their blinders. Without fear, the burden of a monstrous supernatural being is relieved. The relief that comes with the realization that a brutal Sky Fuehrer does not exist is incredible. For the first time in their lives, people who have found enlightenment can think what they want to think and do what they want to do without the constant worry of being punished for eternity.

One successful attorney in a small southern town spent most of his life as a devout Christian. He raised a Christian family and they attended church every Sunday and contributed to the church. His son became an ordained minister. As an attorney, he dealt with reason, logic, evidence, and proof every day in the courtroom. Folklore, superstition, and mythology were not permitted during a trial and were not grounds for convicting someone of a crime. Eventually, this prominent attorney realized that the rules in our legal system should apply to life in general, especially religion. When he attempted to use reason, logic, evidence, and proof in the house of the holy, the lights went out. Today, this outstanding citizen lives a life free from the constraints of an evil god.

A well-known surgeon spent his entire career operating on patients with various diseases and injuries. Although he claimed to be a religious man throughout his life and worshiped a supernatural god, he had reality constantly hitting him in the face. How could a loving, caring god allow a six-year-old boy to develop an inoperable brain tumor? How could this all-powerful deity stand by and ignore the desperate parents praying for a miracle? The doctor finally realized that his loving god did not exist. It was he, not god, who saved the lives of patients. It was his skill and training that saved a person from a life-threatening injury or illness, not god's mercy. Even when the surgeon asked god to help him through a delicate operation, there was no response.

While many use religion to explain their ignorance of the universe and their wish for a better life, neither ignorance nor hope is as strong as fear. Fortunately, many people overcome this fear and live long fulfilled lives without constantly worrying about an evil, supernatural being. But unfortunately, many never get over the fear that was instilled in them in childhood.

THOU SHALT NOT LIE

One of the laws of god in the Ten Commandments is, "Thou Shalt Not Lie." The religious folks insist that the Commandments be posted on the walls of schools, courtrooms, and other public buildings. Apparently just telling people that lying is wrong is not good enough. A constant reminder and the threat of god's wrath seem necessary to get the point across.

One must ask why there is not a disclaimer in the Commandments that reads, "One Must Strictly Follow These Rules To Make God Happy, But If A few Are Broken, You May Still Go To Heaven If You Say 'I'm Sorry', And Believe In Jesus Christ." Quite a few devout followers use this "Get out of Jail Free" card to their advantage. (Al Capone and Hitler come to mind.)

One of the contradictions in the teaching of Christian tradition is the lies told to our children concerning religious holidays. For some reason, the national holidays celebrating the birth, death, and resurrection of Jesus are the ones filled with the greatest amount of lying. The myths of Santa Claus and the Easter Bunny, which seem harmless on the surface, are nothing more than Christians telling lies to their children. These traditions are fun and do little harm, but at the same time they are filled with the sin of lying.

Why does lying seem to be acceptable during Easter and Christmas? Perhaps god waives the rules during the holidays.

> I am the almighty Yahweh. Do not lie. Lying is a sin. You will go to hell for lying. Do not make me mad, for I do tend to have somewhat of an inability to control my temper. I spare no mercy. However, I will waive lying on holidays if you worship my only boy while you are lying. And don't forget to mention me. I need praise, too!

Most religious folks do not consider it lying when they tell their young ones that a jolly old man with a white beard and a red suit lives at the North Pole and spends all year making billions of toys for the good children of the world. They also think it is perfectly normal to tell these innocent toddlers that this fellow flies around the globe in a sleigh pulled by reindeer and manages to visit every house on earth in a single night. When questioned, the pious respond that these little white lies are harmless. They feel that brainwashing their children with such stupidity is all in fun and is part of a longstanding religious tradition.

If anyone is interested in how a first-grader in school can immediately become public enemy number one and be ostracized and ridiculed by the class, one author (CG) will be glad to tell you. Simply walk into class one bright December morning and boldly proclaim, "There is no Santa Claus!"

Talk about getting people's attention! Anyway, it's really not all that bad eating lunch by yourself and not getting picked by the kickball team. Besides, spending recess alone under a shady pine tree can be very inspirational. Also, it was good training for this individual for the future when several years later, he walked into Sunday school class and stated, "There is no God!" Or why not try blurting out, "Jesus wasn't born on December 25th." The Christians needed to take over the Winter Solstice. We do not know any biblical scholar who believes that Jesus was born on December 25th.

It is interesting to note that young children eventually outgrow their beliefs in Santa Claus, the Easter Bunny, and the Tooth Fairy. As they become older, wiser, and more logical, they realize these characters are only make-believe and cannot possibly exist. Choosing to stop believing in the unbelievable is easy for most youngsters because they fear no punishment for not believing. Logic and reasoning override fantasy and allow for intellectual thought to prevail. However, if a disbelief in Santa resulted in going to hell, there would be several million intelligent adults leaving milk and cookies at the fireplace for Jolly Old Saint Nick on Christmas Eve. Fear will always supersede logic and reason. Christians claim that atheists insult their intelligence, but in truth, Christians insult their own intelligence with fear and superstition.

Religious followers walk through their lives with blinders. They preach the Ten Commandments to whoever will listen, with no awareness that those commandments placed restrictions on how a Jew could treat a fellow Jew. They did not restrict the way Jews treated non-Jews. Most people apply God's rules only when it is convenient and does not impose any burden on their lifestyles. Most act as though the commandments are for someone else, not for them. After all, they are going to heaven regardless of what they do during their brief visit on earth. They do not have to follow the Ten Commandments since Jesus has already suffered for their sins and guaranteed their way to heaven.

John F. Kennedy wrote, "The great enemy of truth is very often not the lie – deliberate, contrived, and dishonest – but the myth – persistent, persuasive, and unrealistic."

CHRISTIAN LOVE

Annie Laurie Gaylor is the co-director of the Freedom From Religion Foundation (FFRF) based in Madison, Wisconsin. She is a beautiful person inside and out and is well liked and loved by all who know her. Recently she was interviewed on the Paula Zahn CNN Show and on the O'Reilly Factor Fox program. She was allowed to express her thoughts concerning religion and god. After the airing of the programs, she received many comments, mail, and e-mails. With the permission of FFRF we print these corresponding comments from America's good, caring, god-loving Christians.

BEWARE OF FOUL LANGUAGE BY GOOD CHRISTIANS

(Names are omitted to protect the guilty)

Fuck you

Fuck you…we are founded on judeo-christian values no room here for your bullshit new vogue ideas what the fuck are you thinking?(K.B.)

Annie go f-yourself

Just saw you on O'reilly and you can go f-yourself! If you don't like our country Go live somewhere else perhaps Iraq. (C.C.)

You're A Sick Bitch

You're a complete moron if you can't seem to understand the constitution of the United States that scum like you are trying to debase. All you liberal bitch's, along with the homosexual ACLU scum should be lined up against the wall. I, along with 85% 0f this country would support the candidate that goes after you commi bastards. Go watch a porno of your mother you sick bastards. ("Private Eye's")

How do you people sleep at night?

How about "Freedom from idiots like you?" You are outnumbered by believers and always will be. Find a country to live in where you can do whatever you want. (C.C.)

You are disgusting.

You don't deserve to live in this nation. ("mred")

You can all go to hell.

You all can go to hell since you don't believe in God. I suggest you move to a satan loving country or just somewhere besides the USA WHERE THE COUNTRY WAS FOUNDED IN THE BELIEF OF GOD. WHY DON'T YOU ALL JUST GET A LIFE A LIFE FILLED W/THE JOY OF JESUS!! (J.B.)

God Bless America

You make me vomit and sick and I pray to GOD that you go to hell. (W.C.)

Freedum

Please keep your opinions out of Peoria, Illinois. Contrary to your organizations thinking, we need to put more religion into our government just as our forefathers did. (R.E.)

Eau Claire

I am so sick and tired of you phonies bastardizing the constitution and the first amendment. Enough is enough. Here is my message for Annie Laurie Gaylor. Grab your ankles and go fuck yourself! (T.W.)

How dare You People

How dare you people while standing up for your religious rights you people are trying to take away the rights of believing Christians. We got her some how and it certainly wasn't by emactulant conception. This notion was created by GOD it belongs to GOD so leave it alone!!!!!!!! (A.H.)

Freedom from religion

If you go to Russia, then you can have freedom from religion. America does not need your kind here, would you please leave and never return. Americans wants religion in all parts of our lives, if you don't then leave. (R.P.)

The real enemy

I just saw your interview on tv. Our countrys' foundations are in Christianity. Now we know who the real enemy is to our contry (D.)

"Full of Crap"

Madam: After having just seen you on television, wish to communicate the following thoughts to you – I must say that you are "Full of Crap."

You, and an infinitessilmally small number of self-centered ass-holes – would like to change the world! UP YOURS –IDIOTS! (R.M.)

Good show on Oreilly

Listen you cunt, now that I have your attention listen up scum bitch. Who the fuck at you to tell anyone what they can and cant do? Fuck you. Fuck you and your anti-Christmas agenda. You and a subhuman degenerate waste of human DNA and should be exiled to France. Have you nothing better to do with your worthless life. Go get a real job, even at McDonalds flipping burgers you degenerate whore. (R.V.)

Move to Cuba

You make me sick. Move to Cuba. Merry Christmas. (G.V.)

Factor Appearance

Ms. Gaylor: A lot of us are getting tired of being the repressed majority. (S.C.)

Fox news interview

You are pathetic. You need to get a life, and if you don't like Christmas, then get the hell out of the U.S. And take your beliefs with you. I am tired to idiots like you in our country. And maybe sign up for other unconstitutional organizations, like idiots smoking in private business. Or gays against war. You type of people are not Americans and I don't want you protesting in America, when you are gutless to begin with. (C.)

FFRF

You are a pathetic bitch! (D.E.)

Anti-American morons
You are all a bunch of anti-American morons. (J.N.)

Banning Religious Holidays
Go Fuck yourself! (T.M.)
P.S. Your Bitch on fox news is an idiot

Christmas & God in School
I was just sickened by your spokes "woman" on Fox News and just would like to say one thing…it's all about people like you that have contributed to the communist idea and the demise of America. I hope you will at least realize, at your death, how wrong you are before you end up in Hell as well! It makes me want to puke looking and listening to people like you! (C.H.)

Christian-based Country
This country was founded by Christians. …Satan knows his time is up…he is trying desperately to pull as many people from God as he can, including people from your organization. Whatever your activity, leading people from God, will be punished at the end of your life. (P.Y.)

Unrepentantly sub-human
I was just flipping through the channels tonight, when I happened upon The O'Reily Factor'. It is good to have a name and a face to put on the enemy. Your closed-minded bigotry is so unrepentantly sub-human. Have a meaningless, soulless, organic day. (D.S.)

Anne Laurie Taylor on O'Reilly
Fuck the double ugly bitch and fuck all of you atheists scum. There are no atheists in Foxholes. What a sick bunch of bastards. You worthless lying politician whores

and sluts, tell me one religion that has been established. This is one fucked up organization of communist and hatemongers. Maybe most of you scum anti Americans imbeciles will rot in hell. (J.M.)

Ms. Gaylor

I was amazed at Ms. Gaylor's display this evening on Fox. She would do well to join the Cindy Sheehans of the world. (M.D.)

You are a disgrace

You are sick. I just saw a program on Fox TV and I could not believe your stupidity! Why don't you just leave this great country that was founded on religious beliefs! If you don't like it just try Russia or China for instance! You are a disgrace to our country, or schools, our churches, our people, our world!!!! YOU ARE SICK!!! (L.M.)

Your deceit

On November 21st I watched Fox News and witnessed Annie Laurie Gaylor speak of your organization. The issue of separation of church and state has been blown completely way from its original meaning. I think, as time goes on, that you will learn the true meaning of backlash. Lots of us are really getting extremely angry with the nonsense you stand for. (J.H.)

Hannity and comes

I think you will soon be out of the litigation business when Judge Alito gets on the supreme court. The court will then be set for many years to come and faith based programs will accelerate and take over our country. I guess then our country will go back to what it was founded on.....the true Gospel of Jesus Christ. (G.F.)

Interviews

I suppose that you, along with the lesbian led NOW want to change history. (K.H.)

Target ban

I bet you're a drunken whore. (R.H.)

You Are Commmie Bastards

You and the ACLU should be ashamed of yourself , and should be shipped out of this country, to some place that is stupid enough to believe in the KRAP you are spreading! (M.B.)

Atheist traditions

You people should be ashamed. I just heard some nut on fox talk about atheist traditions, which there are none!!!! (M.K.)

Scum of the earth

You Ms Gaylor, and people LIKE you are the scum of America. Ane if you are going to appear on any more talk shows, I would consider some plastic surgery and perhaps some dental work! (P.D.)

Mr. Barker and fellow Druids,

I read with interest your contribution to the "holiday" exhibits in the Wisconsin rotunda. May the Holy Spirit penetrate your hardened hearts so that you might know the joy of our Saviour's birth, life, crucifixion, and resurrection to that you won't have to spend eternity separated from the God you chose to deny. (J.W.)

Stoned to Death

People like you who interpret the bible wrong and try to sell this BS to people should be "stoned to death" (N.N.)

Christians tirelessly promote the notion that god loves us, Jesus loves us, and that they (i.e., the Christians) love us. When you love someone, you don't hate that person. Let us examine the above comments from this perspective.

Obscene and vulgar language: We do not use obscene and vulgar language towards the people we love. When we do so in anger, we recover and apologize profusely. Whether we are god-fearing or not, most of us know that the use of such language, especially towards strangers, is simply wrong. An interesting side point is that Christians are usually the first ones to be offended by the obscenities and vulgarities used in popular culture. Periodically they demand that the entertainment industry clean up its act and affix some kind of rating so that people will know that a movie, TV show, or a song contains obscenities. It is interesting that they then turn around and use this kind of language in a public discourse.

The church and its religious leaders should start another crusade – this time towards their own followers: Clean up your language; be respectful of other people and their opinions; refrain from using hateful language; respect the fundamental freedom of expression by people from all walks of life.

Notice the use of capital letters and the use of multiple exclamation points in the above posts. It is generally understood that when someone writes a sentence or a paragraph in all capital letters that that person is screaming at someone. We wish that these

Christians would talk to people with love rather than scream at them in anger. We also wish that these self-described Christians, as alleged beneficiaries of god's love, calmly talk to people and express their opinions in a reasonable manner so that a meaningful dialogue can be held. It is impossible to communicate when one of the parties is screaming obscenities.

The idea of a wall between the church and the state seems to rile a lot of Christians. The idea of separation of church and state was conceived for the benefit of all Christian denominations. At the time of the drafting of the Constitution, there was a real danger that the states and the local governments would impose a religious litmus test – e.g., an office holder must belong to a specified denomination such as an Anglican or a Presbyterian Church. Denominations such as the Methodist Church and the Mormon Church did not exist at the time of the Revolution. Baptists were a small minority. There was a real fear among smaller denominations that they would be swallowed up or suppressed by the use of governmental power. Notice that the first Catholic person to be elected to the office of the President of the United States did not occur until the second half of the twentieth century – until then being a Catholic was an automatic disqualification for election to a high office. Jews, of course, have always been in a precarious position. The wall of separation between the church and state, thus, was enunciated to alleviate the anxieties of these denominations. Most of the correspondents who were abusive to Annie Laurie Gaylor forgot about the rationale that governments need to stay out of religious business. On top of that, they want to use the government to promote their agendas. There is good reason to be afraid of the establishment of religious tyranny.

It must be emphasized over and over that religion is only as good as the people who practice it. If people's beliefs make them more kind, tolerant, and charitable, then those beliefs are worthwhile. But faith in an afterlife does not justify such Christian love as depicted in the above letters. We have only to read the daily newspaper to see the same hatred, bigotry, and insanity by the believers of Islam.

While we can only hope that the sentiments expressed by the above Christian letter writers do not represent those of most Christians, they nevertheless are examples of the effects of religion on large numbers of believers.

We must ask, "What is it that makes Christians like the above so cruel, hateful, and bigoted? Why do the churches and their pastors not speak out against such behavior?" The answer is simple: without absolute dogma that allows no questioning, beliefs in the supernatural cannot be sustained.

The Ten Commandments need to be rewritten. The first commandment should be, "You shall be responsible for your own actions." The second commandment should be, "You shall do no harm in the name of god."

WOMAN

Women historically have held goddess positions. The Greek god Zeus allowed Aphrodite to serve as the goddess of beauty and sexual desire; Hestia got the important role as the home and hearth goddess; the Egyptian goddess Ernutet was in charge of women in childbirth. Many early belief systems included females in their hierarchy of divine rulers.

However, after the big discovery around 3500 BCE that children had fathers, few women made it to the top position. The Great Spirit in the sky was invariably a male. He was a hard charging, revengeful, egocentric, and testosterone-driven male who ruled the universe with an iron fist. These types of rulers still exist today. The JCM god and the Taliban are good examples of these characters. Women are assigned lesser roles in heaven and on earth.

A direct result of the dominant male god is that it encouraged men to put women in subordinate positions for thousands of years. This male chauvinistic attitude began when men, not women, invented and reinvented religion. By placing the blame of this dominant anti-female stance on his newly invented male god, man could go about his daily business treating women like doormats and getting away with it.

One would think that as we progressed from an ancient Greek religion into a single god religion, the plight of women would have improved. In actuality, it got worse. The new modern Abrahamic Jewish religion conveniently left women out completely. All of the books in the Bible were written by men. Why weren't women invited to participate in the creation of this religious text? Were they just too uneducated to read and write? Or perhaps men thought that women were not credible enough to attest to the miracles of god and his son. One would think that a book as important as the ineffable word of god would have at least a few female authors. But none are to be found among the male authors posing as Moses, Solomon, Matthew, Mark, Luke, John, and Paul, as well as many others. There is not a single verse is this holy book written by a woman. It is obvious that this religion was created by males for males, and for males' needs. God was so macho that males were created first. "So god made man like his maker. Like god, did god make man…to be the masters of all life upon the earth and in the skies and in the seas." Genesis 1: 26. God went on to say, "It isn't good for the man to be alone; I will make a helper suited to his needs." Genesis 2: 18. When Adam was confronted with eating the forbidden fruit, he told god it was Eve's fault and god believed it.

> Hey god, don't blame me! It was that woman you made for me. It's all her fault. She did it. I'm innocent…after all I am supreme, right god? Sure, son. I'll punish Eve, instead. Woman, you shall bear children in intense pain and suffering; yet even so, you shall

> welcome your husband's affections
> and he shall be your master.

Apparently Eve accepted the guilt that god imposed upon her without question because soon after this divine scolding she jumped into bed with Adam. Nothing has changed since. While we are on the subject, does anyone know where Cain's wife came from? A little incest here?

Women have served men for thousands of years due to ancient superstitions and fears. Millions of highly intelligent women still walk behind their man with their faces covered with cloth. If the uglier of the two faces has to be covered, one would think it would be the male wearing the veil. But such is not the case. Other practices, such as women not being allowed to dine with men or not being allowed in business or politics, all have their roots based on religion. It is hard to imagine that less than a hundred years ago women could not vote in America. Pay scales have historically been less for women even when performing the same duties as men. Fortunately, America's "glass ceiling" is slowly breaking down.

No discussion on the debasing of women would be complete without mentioning the Age of Chivalry during the Middle Ages. Christian men used the chastity belt to prevent their wives from having sex while they were away on the Crusades killing the Muslims. Those humiliating devices were locked with a key and were extremely uncomfortable for the hapless woman. Many women wore chastity belts for years while awaiting the return of their crusading husbands. There is no evidence however, that the lascivious warrior maintained chaste while he was away. After all, the heavy armor could be removed instantly should the need arise. And one can assume that the need often arose. There is the tale of the crusader leaving the key to the chastity belt with his most trusted friend. Shortly after the crusader rode off, his friend rode up to him on horseback and exclaimed, "You left the wrong key."

Sex in biblical times as it is today was a major issue. Women were accused of sexual misconduct more often than men. Adulterous men, at worst, were reprimanded or scolded. A man could pretty much do as he wanted when it came to his sexual prowess. After all, he was considered the lion looking out at his pride. Take whichever one you want and have your way with her to satisfy your needs, not hers. Women, however, were not allowed the discretion of random sex. The woman who behaved sexually like a man was called a whore and a sinner, and the punishment for such behavior was death by stoning.

Thousands of years have passed and the terms whore and tramp are still used for women, but not for men. Modern women still abide by the double standard and the ancient rules imposed in the Bible. A woman must serve the man and remain subservient. Christian books for women written in the 20th century stress that adulterous behavior in husbands is caused by the wife. Bad hygiene and lack of sexual desire causes a man to cheat on his wife. It's not the man's fault, woman, it's yours! Straighten up and keep yourself clean, and maybe your gallivanting husband will come home. And when he finally does come back, forgive him. He's been through a lot. It's not his fault, it's yours.

Many Christian men have committed adultery as the word is now commonly understood. It originally meant the fraudulent impregnation of a married woman, thereby robbing her legal owner of his right to pass on his inheritance to his biological heir. Their religion did not hold them accountable for such behavior outside their tribe. They knew their wives were not going to do the same thing because that would make them whores and send them straight to hell. What a deal for the man! If he got caught, a simple visit to church for confession would cleanse the penitent man and put him back on the pathway to heaven. Why would anyone want to be a woman? It's great being a man. Let the woman have all the pain. After all, it was a woman who ate the forbidden fruit. Men were only forbidden from copulating with a fellow Jew's wife and violation of that taboo carried the death penalty for both offenders. Numbers 5: 11-31.

Numbers 5: 11-31 describes a test that a jealous and suspecting husband could have performed to prove his wife's adultery. The woman is brought to a priest with an offering of a tenth of a bushel of barley meal without oil or frankincense mingled with it. This offering brings out the guilt. The priest takes her before Yahweh and mixes holy water and dust with the flour. She is handed this potion to drink and if she is innocent, nothing happens. If she is guilty, Yahweh will make a curse among her people as well as making her thigh rot away and cause her body to swell. So ladies be careful. If your husband brings home a tenth of a bushel of barley meal, you just might not be having a good day. Biblical science at work!

Due to thousands of years of sexual prejudice that religion has imposed upon women, they have not been allowed to appreciate one of life's most precious and purest forms of pleasure. Many young Christian girls in America bear the brunt of their parents' and clergy's admonitions when it comes to sex. They are taught that sex is bad. They are taught that it is the only thing boys want. They are taught in church that they will go to hell if they engage in sex before marriage. The threats come from all directions and before these young girls reach puberty they have developed a distorted view of a human function that can be both pleasurable and reproductive.

Consequently, many women spend their entire lives wearing sexual blinders. Sex is bad, nasty, and sinful. Enjoy sex? Never! How can one possibly enjoy something condoned by the devil? The preachers either do not know or they ignore the fact that if sex had not been pleasurable for women in the millennia, the human race would have long ago become extinct. At least women have one thing going for them – their religion made the devil a male, although women were made the devil's sidekicks in the form of witches.

Many young women refrain from premarital sex because of their fear of pregnancy as much as the instilled fear of the devil. As curiosity and tension build, they become eager to marry. When they think they have met Mr. Right, the trip to the altar results. They eagerly rush to the bedroom only to discover how sexually incompatible they are. Unfortunately the damage has already been done. The years of brainwashing have worked its course. She is now in an unhappy marriage and her religious convictions will not allow her to understand or enjoy her own sexuality. Many women remain in miserable marriages due to their religious convictions – convictions that were forced upon them as young girls by their parents and clergy.

Sexual problems develop early in many marriages. Males do not have the same religious restraints as women. They learn at an early age about the enjoyment of sex. King Solomon, one of god's all-time favorites, had seven hundred wives to produce heirs, and three hundred concubines. Wow! All with god's approval. Talk about group sex – Kings 4: 29 states, "God gave Solomon great wisdom and understanding, and a mind with broad interest." You can say that again – 1000 broads.

Women have not had the same divine blessing when it comes to multiple partners. If a woman decides to have two husbands at the same time, she is automatically guilty of bigamy. She will be shunned by society, family, and church. How dare a woman have two husbands! Any woman who copulates with more than one man is considered a tramp and a whore. And lo and behold, if she has seven hundred husbands she would surely be hanging from the same tree that the Christians used for witches. After all, both whores and witches are the products of Satan. One can only wonder why a loving god has allowed this madness to continue.

> Is this really your policy, god? If it is, how about an explanation? Is this

how you treat Mrs. God? Oh, there is no Mrs. God. I see. You say you don't like women? Let up some, god. Eve said she was sorry…what else do you want? Haven't you punished women long enough with your childbearing pain and suffering? Why not give up your anger towards females and let them be equal to men. After all, it is the women of the world who drag their cheating and unfaithful husbands to church every Sunday and make them throw money into your offering plate.
No Reply

Quality sex begins with two consenting equal partners. Nothing drains sexual enjoyment like religious inhibitions. One can only imagine the torment a woman experiences when she thinks an all-knowing, angry god is present in her bedroom and watching every move. This fear is unrealistic, but it exists in many women. Men tend not to worry if god is watching them. They are going to enjoy themselves regardless of what god thinks. Just ask Jim Bakker, Jimmy Swaggart, or Ted Haggard. A woman who can put aside her inhibitions can be a satisfied individual. Forget sin. Forget punishment. Forget all the brainwashing that occurred as a child and enjoy yourself. Couples who mutually enjoy sex are willing and capable of discounting ancient superstitions and myths.

Many women realize that there is nothing sinful about lust. It is a natural function and is nothing to be ashamed of. Modern women are taking control of their sexuality and exercising the same rights that men have had for thousand of years. They are becoming less and less submissive to men solely because of ancient scripture. Sex is no longer a duty for Christian women. It is a privilege to be exercised with prudence and pleasure. It is women's right to control their bodies in reproductive functions through birth control methods. All humans should consider sexually transmitted diseases, unwanted pregnancies, family values, and personal values when engaging in sexual activities.

The authors are not in any way condoning immoral, adulterous, or dangerous sexual behavior. However, both men and women should have the same sexual privileges. Religions should not dictate otherwise.

THE MEANING OF LIFE

Many believers in the JCM god have convinced themselves that their supernatural god gives meaning to their lives. That belief allows them to justify whatever they decide to do. Rationalization allows people to convince themselves that god wants them to do what they finally decide to do with their lives. Fortunately, most of the people who believe this choose worthwhile careers and lifestyles. Not many serial killers and rapists write books about god's meaning in their lives.

The god-given meaning of an individual's life always ends exactly as the individual has decided. If one becomes a preacher, god meant that; if one becomes a physician, god meant that; if one has an opportunity to pastor a larger church for a larger salary, god meant that; if one decides to become a missionary, god meant that. For the fundamentalists, everything they decide to do, god meant for them to do it.

Fortunately for god, he doesn't get the blame for giving people a mean streak or for becoming a psychopathic killer. In truth, the meaning of life varies with one's age and circumstances. Children have little meaning in their lives except to play and grow older. Although these children supposedly have souls, apparently god has not yet put any meaning into their lives. In fact, thanks to early death, many children never mature beyond eating, playing, and sleeping. As children age into puberty the meaning of their lives changes as the girls begin looking at the boys and the boys begin to lust after the girls.

As children advance into adulthood they gradually get the "meaning" that they must find a way to make a living, perhaps even marry and start a family. Never-to-fear, at that time god puts a vocation into their minds and they decide to become chemists, physicists, preachers, and so on.

It should be obvious that the meaning of one's life depends upon one's situation and has no relationship to a supernatural being. If you are addicted to cocaine, the meaning of life is to get the next hit; if you are addicted to religion, the meaning of your life is to make everyone believe as you do; if your life is in peril, the meaning of your life is to become safe; if you are in pain, the meaning of your life is to be rid of it.

We could laugh at the notion that god gives meaning to life were it not for the harm it causes. This notion allows people to escape the responsibility for their actions and decisions; it demeans good people who are acting in the best interest of society by giving god credit for their good works. Neither of these attitudes is conducive to establishing a responsible humane society.

How convenient it is for the religionists to give credit to their god for whatever they decide to do. And how convenient it is for god to get credit for what good people accomplish and get no blame for the socially unacceptable things that people do.

In the final analysis, people must accept the responsibility for their own decisions and actions. The meaning of one's life must rest with the individual. Blaming it on god or giving god the credit is self-defeating and harmful to human society.

There would be more worthwhile meaning in people's lives if they would work for the benefit of humankind instead of for the benefit of a supernatural deity.

RELIGION AT THE CROSSROADS

Religion in America is at a crossroad. Religion can continue with its concerns and worries about pleasing an omniscient, omnipotent god that can get anything it wants whenever it wants it, or it can focus on the concerns of humanity, the animal kingdom, and the earth's environment.

Most religions, especially the JCM religions, are god-centered. These god-centered religions must decide whether they are to continue serving a supernatural being or whether they are to serve humankind. Historically, they have only served a supernatural being. Humans will have to decide if it is even possible that a loving creator would actually expect its children to worship it and make sacrifices to it, and then punish them severely if they do not. Loving parents do not expect such from their children. In fact, parents are usually the ones doing the worshiping and sacrificing for *their* children. This is a natural phenomenon known as true love, an element that seems to be missing in god.

The many religions of the world today, with their large numbers of uneducated, poverty stricken followers are causing untold conflicts, hatred, and wars throughout the world. They are under the leadership of clergy and politicians who seek power, wealth, and control. Religions can continue in that vein – and no doubt some will – or they can accept the fact that the universe and first cause are unknown mysteries that are yet to be solved. They may say as did Galileo, "I know it not," and strive for truth.

Religions and governing bodies as well as all organized groups must take the path of service for the common good of humankind. Human morality and human laws must be established by humans for humans. Gods can fight their own battles. Man must fight man's battles. Organized groups including religions and service clubs as well as local, state, and national governments, must be instrumental in the preservation and well-being of humankind and the earth's environment. Some of these groups serve those needs today, but many religious and governmental groups serve only the needs of their own power structure. They serve the needs of their constituents only as it serves the institution that they control. This causes competition and constant power struggles between the groups. The "trickle down" theory only works if there is a flood. Many times aid in the form of money does little good when it is passed through people's hands with sticky fingers. The "after me, you come first" folks in power let little trickle down.

Organized religion with its historical quest for power is now at the crossroads of serving god or serving humanity. Some religions have already taken the path for humanity. They have de-emphasized a mysterious god that no one understands or can describe. They realize that service to mankind is foremost and that worshiping god is secondary. Some religions keep their fear of god, but play it down as they try to serve their constituents' needs. People coming together as a group can better organize and serve humanity than an individual. However, it must never be forgotten that while one individual may not have the power and resources to do everything, he/she should do what he/she is able to do. While this concept is simple and elementary, it is nevertheless true and important and bears repeating.

We can only hope that more organized religions will take the path of service to humanity. Church and State must remain separate and a distinct wall must be maintained between them. Those serving god must never be allowed to interfere with those serving their fellow man. Hopefully America will follow some of the European nations and remove ancient superstition from modern jurisprudence. For civilization to survive, man will have to be governed by logic, reason, and intelligence – not by antiquated dogma, sorcery, witchcraft, and make-believe demons. No civilization in history has failed because it was too reasonable. Future generations will not tolerate leaders governing their nations on the basis of pious tenets. A president who even hints that he or she has had a conversation with god will likely be removed from office. Today people who have conversations with god are certifiably insane.

For churches to survive they must become forces for the betterment of humanity and become more involved in secular projects of helping humankind. They cannot depend on or wait on the supernatural for assistance. When humans finally realize that praying for divine intervention does not work, has never worked and never will work, they will turn to their fellow man for answers and solutions, and leave the gods where they belong – locked away in the places of worship. People will become more humanistic and less theistic. The sooner we realize that we and only we are responsible for ourselves, the sooner we will enjoy a world without conflict.

Yogi Berra said, "When you come to a fork in the road, take it." Hopefully, religions will take the road to serving humanity, not god.

JUDGING GOD

Religions and gods have been judging man for thousands of years. It is about time for man to judge god. No god, religion, president, dictator, or scientific theory should ever be above criticism and evaluation. Truth is the only sacred thing. In this book we have been judging the JCM god, a god believed by billions.

For thousands of years people have been terrified by the claim that we are constantly being watched and judged by god. According to this belief god watches our every move (although he seemed to have lost Adam and Eve in the Garden of Eden) and keeps a thorough record of our behavior during our short stay on earth. At the end of this brief stay, god and only god decides whether we will go to an eternity in the scorching heat of hell or the glorious paradise of heaven.

We are not afforded a fair trial by jury; we are not offered a defense attorney; we do not even have the right to make a statement on our own behalf. The bottom line is that god is the prosecutor, jury, and judge wrapped in one package and he has no respect for the concept of habeas corpus or a fair trial. At least the infamous "Hangin' Judge" Roy Bean allowed his defendants to make a statement before they were hung.

We are taught by the clergy that the law of god takes precedence over the law of man, regardless of what our earthbound mortal judges decide. According to this belief, our fate is determined by the judgment of god.

To become a judge in America one has to meet impeccable standards. A potential judge must undergo stringent scrutiny regarding morals, ethics, wisdom, emotional stability, and character. Defendants in a court of law can rest assured that their case will be heard and evaluated based on logic, reason, prudence, and evidence.

According to scripture, Judgment Day is the day when each individual will be judged and sentenced to hell or heaven. If the sentence is hell, one can be certain it will be life without parole.

Imagine for a moment a defendant in a court being tried for robbery. Although he may be aware that his crime deserves punishment, he is also aware that his judge is the most heinous, vicious, and brutal serial killer humankind has ever experienced. This judge has murdered millions of innocent people – not in a painless way as Hitler gassed the Jews – but in an even more horrid manner of drowning. This judge showed no mercy on millions of his own children as he annihilated babies and children whose only desire in life was to play in the back yard. He condoned the raping of women, mutilation of the elderly, and the total destruction of their homes and cities. This biblical judge encouraged looting and stealing from those he did not like. This judge has a history of mental illness as he cannot control his temper and is jealous of other judges. He is easily persuaded to change his mind; he is revengeful; he cannot keep his emotions in check; his wrath is unprecedented.

But, he is the judge! The god that is determining our destiny is less qualified to conduct court than the lowest bottom feeder in the chain of humanity.

It is time for man to become the judge of god. We must put aside our fears and call god to the courtroom. As decent, reasonable humans we will give god a fair trial, complete with legal representation and a panel of impartial jurors. God could pick any defense attorney he desires. He could call Saint Peter and get a list of resident attorneys, although that list might be quite short in heaven.

God should be called to the stand and required to tell the truth, "So help me Humanity." He would be required to explain the flood and why he killed all human and animal life on earth, except for those on the ark. He would be given the opportunity to justify the plagues, disasters, fires, famines, and other atrocities that he has imposed upon helpless humans. Perhaps with a good defense attorney, god could convince the jury why he brutally killed thousands of Christians while trying to obliterate a few gays in New Orleans. Perhaps the defense team will bring out viable reasons why all the first-born male children were slaughtered in Egypt. There may even be an acceptable reason why god destroyed the city of Jericho and all of its inhabitants. Who knows, god's version of what happened thousands of years ago may completely contradict the tales in the Bible. At least he would be given an opportunity to explain his actions as they were recorded in the Bible.

In addition to all of the direct killings, god should be held accountable for birth defects, disease, natural disasters, famine, poverty, and the senseless wars he has created to pit humans against one another. In essence, the jury must decide if god has lived up to the same standards as humanity. If our almighty creator and ruler cannot exceed the morals, ethics, and values of humanity, he should be removed from office and never allowed to control humankind again.

We should be asking, "What kind of job is god doing?" Religions and their leaders have been successful in preventing people from judging their gods by calling such people blasphemers, heretics, infidels, or secular humanists as if sanity, intelligence, and education could cause immorality rather that deter it. If that does not keep them quiet, shun them, excommunicate them, ruin their business, run them out of town – even kill them.

As hatred, bigotry, cruelty, and killing continue in god's name, it is obvious that something has gone awry. One must either be unwilling to think or terrified of death to believe what people claim to be god's commandments. The hundreds of bibles and the millions of people who say they are speaking for god make god look like an indecisive cruel monster rather than a loving god. We cannot determine what god is responsible for, or if it is responsible for anything. In fact, god is so vague and nebulous that it is hard to believe that a loving, personal, supernatural being exists. There is no evidence that god is tending to his creations, as the big animals continue to eat the little animals and many species of plants and animals have become extinct and other species of plants and animals are rapidly dwindling. Most believers cannot determine who is responsible for evil, god or the devil, or if they are simply eye-of-the-beholder interpretations of the same blind men's elephant.

If god really wants people to believe in his existence, we venture to make a few suggestions. First, god should tell all the occupants of the universe exactly what he wants and requires. This information should be communicated directly to each and every person on earth in such a manner that it cannot be misunderstood. He should stop using messengers such as the late Jerry Falwell, John the Baptist, Jesus, and Muhammad to spread his word. These types of characters would benefit man more by becoming comedians on Comedy Central rather than spokespersons for an almighty god. An omnipotent, omniscient supernatural being needs no spokespersons. It should speak for itself.

Secondly, god needs to inform people as to why he is making demands on them. His demands must make sense to the cognitive mind. He should explain in detail what the big problem is with uncircumcised penises. Why does god have to worry about such mundane issues? One would think that millions of starving children in the world would take priority over a little foreskin. For those who maintain that god is love, he has a strange way of showing it.

Let us now make some more suggestions as to how an omnipotent being could prove that it exists. If god were to tell everyone exactly what day the Sabbath is and exactly what can and cannot be done on the Sabbath, then on the following Sabbath kill all those who didn't do as he commanded, that would be proof positive. This seems somewhat cruel according to human standards, but then again, no crueler than what is now being done in his name. Or, how about throwing a tsunami fit or generating a big earthquake one day, killing thousands of folks and causing massive destruction to their homes and habitat? Then, the next day or the third day or the seventh day restore everything, including people's lives, just as they were before the disaster. That would be proof positive to all but the totally insane that god existed and that he is all-powerful and should be listened to and obeyed.

As we watched millions of people praying for the dying Pope, we thought that if god would only keep the Pope alive and make him young and vigorous again, that would truly be a miracle. If God really liked the guy and let him live for a thousand years or so, everyone would realize that god existed and all would follow his orders. If god allowed Noah, Moses, and other biblical characters to live for six or seven hundred years, why does he kill off the popes before they reach a hundred?

But enough about proving that god exists. We are sure that with god's knowledge and power, he can think of many ways to prove that he exists. He would not have to do it by brutally killing folks. He could pick a few of his devoted followers who have pleased him and give them happiness and goodies that others do not have. For example, he could create golden hotels for the devoted followers and let prepared food appear miraculously every day so that those followers did not have to strain themselves with mundane tasks. When everyone sees how god's devoted followers are blessed, they will automatically follow the example of the blessed.

Torturing and killing would not be necessary – it is old-fashioned and represents decadent and cruel Roman Empire practices. Surely god could be better than those pagan Romans. A loving god would use positive reinforcement, not punishment.

If god cannot make people believe that he exists, how can he possibly expect them to obey his commands? And speaking of commandments, god really needs to clean them up and make them understandable. The thousands of bibles, sacred texts, and orders that emanate in god's name are inane and cruel. Believing in god's vague and conflicting orders and putting them into practice is impossible.

After god proves that he exists, he needs to make it perfectly clear what he expects from people. Some of the religious believers say that god decides human morality, but he has not done a good job of telling us what that morality is. His vague directions on slavery, women's rights, sex, charity, love, and kindness are so conflicting as to make it impossible to determine what he really wants. In the meantime, those who are speaking as his representatives put their own slant on what god wants and prevent logical, reasonable people from deciding and establishing human morality.

When god proclaims, "Thou shall not kill," he should tell us in what situations it is acceptable to kill. After all, god has done a bit of killing himself. Are we not supposed to follow his divine example? If according to the Old Testament it is OK for Jews to kill people of other tribes in Israel, will it be OK for Christians to kill Muslims and for Muslims to kill Jews and Christians? If not, why not? People should hear directly from god as to what happens to those who do not obey.

God, you need to speak up and stop pussyfooting around with your orders. Many if not most of your designated ecclesiastic spokespersons are full of hot air, others are downright con men. They have become rich by spreading your word, even though your own allegedly infallible book states that the rich have difficulty getting into heaven.

Some of us are from Missouri, the show me state – we must be convinced with our own intellect. The least that you can do is to explain what you want in no uncertain terms. Those picayunish miracles that you let Jesus and the Catholics get by with are not impressive. Making wine for a crowd at a wedding is not our idea of a celestial deed. Surely you can come up with some miracles that benefit all of mankind. The alcoholics of the world do not need any more booze, but the millions of starving children would appreciate a little food. At least perform some miracles that would prove an omnipotent, omniscient, supernatural being actually exists. If you have any trouble thinking of some good miracles, we would be happy to make some suggestions. How about a cure for cancer tomorrow? Wave your magic wand and get rid of AIDS.

Once you prove that you exist and are in control, people will do whatever you command. The threat, "If you don't do what I tell you to do, I'll zap you", and then not zap us until after we die does not get the job done. That threat by the clergy does bring in money and keeps the followers in line, but in doing so, it creates a lifetime of fear. We know that a kind and loving god would not want fear for his children.

Sorry god, you do not pass the muster. You have failed miserably in your communication skills. You seem to be angry most of the time. Creating Saint Lucifer, then allowing him to get out of control and wreak havoc on your loving subjects shows poor judgment, ineptness, and incompetence on your part. The methods you have used to prove your love, charity, and kindness, such as allowing your own son to be tortured and killed is a good example of why people fear you, but it does not make people love or respect you. If it is your goal to make everyone terrified of death, you have accomplished that for the majority of people. If your goal is to create a happy and well-fed comfortable humanity, you have failed miserably. What you have accomplished is to allow a bunch of religious fundamentalists to create their own sense of morality and put the blame on you. You must stop communicating through these emotional bigots and start communicating directly with all people on this earth. Do not forget the telephone game where communications get screwed up as they pass from person to person. The least you can do is to start a heavenly newspaper or set up an internet website so that every individual can get information directly from you.

One last thing, god. Why don't you follow the behavior of millions of mothers and fathers around the world who deeply love their children regardless of what the children think about their parents? These devoted parents would never send their children to eternal punishment for not believing in them. In fact, instead of punishing their offspring for not believing, most parents would look inward and try to improve on their own personal failures. Perhaps you could do a little of that yourself.

Like humans, god, if you want respect you must earn it. We judge you by your actions and your deeds just as we judge our fellow man. It is necessary to judge people by what they do, not by what they say. Sorry god, with all due respect, you fail the test. You do not come up to human standards of morality.

GOD'S TRIAL

The first step in due process when someone is accused of a wrongdoing is to present a grand jury with enough evidence to obtain an indictment. If the grand jury believes that the evidence is insufficient for prosecution, the suspect must be released. On the other hand, if the grand jury believes that there is sufficient evidence of wrongdoing, the suspect will be detained and scheduled for trial. All a grand juror would have to do to indict god is to read the Bible.

Once a defendant is charged with wrongdoing, the next step is for the defendant to obtain legal counsel. If god cannot afford an attorney, he will be furnished one at no charge – a benefit that god has never given to the people he has judged. In fact, if a person were to appear at god's trial with an attorney, there is no doubt that both would be led away in chains to await transfer to the inferno of eternity – hell. In contrast to a trial run by god, god would have the right to defend himself at humanity's trial. God will need the best lawyer available to help explain the charges against him. Perhaps Johnnie Cochran is available, although it may be difficult to find him. Surely the Gatekeeper will grant Cochran a temporary pass to defend god.

Step three in the due process of justice is to pick a location for the trial. Criminal trials are usually held where the crime was committed. In this instance however, the alleged crimes were committed in every city, state, and nation in the world. A change of venue is not going to do much good here. God could be extradited to another location in the world, but where? Obviously, only to a place that has never heard of god and his alleged crimes will assure a fair and unbiased trial. Perhaps if we look hard enough there is still an island in the South Pacific where its inhabitants have not heard about god. Unfortunately, this trial may be conducted in a courthouse constructed of bamboo walls, straw roof, and dirt floors. There will probably be no electricity, so CNN, C-Span, and Fox News (if they decide to show up) will have to bring their own generators. As we said, "God, you were promised a fair trial and by humanity, you are going to get one."

Step four in this continuing due process of law is to find a panel of twelve impartial jurors. Both sides of the defense have a say as to who the jurors are. The concept of habeas corpus revolves around the notion that an individual is judged by his peers. These peers, in order to be qualified as jurors, must demonstrate that they are capable of making prudent decisions based solely on the evidence presented and not on a preconceived notion of the defendant's guilt or innocence. Where are we going to find these twelve jurors? Certainly not in New Orleans, Key West, or San Francisco. We also can exclude Egypt and the entire continent of Africa. Descendents from the ancient tribes and nations where god caused plagues, diseases, and destruction are not going to be good jurors either. In fact, many of these descendents are still feeling the effects of god's multi-generational curses that he placed upon their forefathers. It would not be fair for god to have a person so cursed as one of his jurors.

We must also exclude women, homosexuals, and Afro-Americans from the list of potential jurors. God may want them on his jury, but we would highly recommend against it. We really think god would fare better if he did not have a subservient, pregnant, barefoot, and abused woman on his panel of jurors. And please don't insist on a starving, dehydrated, AIDS-infected Sudanese either. Gay men and women might not be appropriate, after what you said about them – perhaps you best leave them out also.

This brings us back to the little island in the South Pacific. This is probably the only place in the world where god can obtain a panel of unbiased jurors who have not experienced the disastrous effects of his jealousy, anger, and wrath. They will listen to the evidence presented and make rational decisions as to the fate of god. God can be assured that he will be given a fair trial. The fact that the jurors and the judge are uneducated and have no access to news of world events and the internet will actually work in his favor. Once again god, we want to emphasize that you are going to get a fair trial.

Once this fair trial commences, god still has a rough road ahead. Most criminals, even the most heinous, take painstaking efforts to cover up their crime. Many killers have been convicted on flimsy evidence. Many more have been acquitted or released on appeal because of insufficient evidence. A motto in the criminal justice system is, "It is better to let a guilty man go free than to punish an innocent one." God for some strange reason documented all of his crimes and then brags about them. He has written a book, *The Living Bible,* where he documents all of his crimes and atrocities against man. He makes no bones about it in his book; he brutally murdered millions of men, women, children, and babies because of his anger and rage. He admits that he has emotional problems; that he is jealous; that he is vengeful; and that he cannot control his temper. God also admits that he is easily influenced by the devil, and in some cases lets the devil take over his decision making. He also admits in his book that he condones slavery, hates homosexuals, and thinks women are nothing more than doormats.

One legal possibility is that god may be judged innocent due to insanity. After all, one *must* be insane to flood the entire world and kill the entire population because of the sins of some of the inhabitants. No sane person would kill all the first-born males of a society. No sane person would kill a person because he saw your face. No sane ruler of the universe would infect millions of starving children with AIDS because he hated gays.

Yes god, we are going to support giving you a fair trial. Unlike you, we are human and humane. We will give you the benefit of the doubt. You will have your day in court, unlike the billions you have sentenced to hell without a trial.

If you are convicted of these crimes, we will promise not to subject you to eternal torture. We realize that you have sent billions of people to hell for minor infractions, but we as humans believe that the punishment should fit the crime and therefore we cannot possibly be as cruel as you. No, we will just remove you from office and incarcerate you in a place that has air-conditioning, cable TV, and three square meals a day. You will have a library, gym, and free medical care – all compliments of humanity. We do not want to torture you as you do to humanity. We just want you off our streets so that the world can be civilized, something you have failed to do.

If and when god understands his faults and his bedeviling psychological problems, we may be able to reconcile our relationship. However, we must emphasize that humankind will no longer tolerate a brutal, violent, and ruthless murderer. Humanity would welcome a peaceful, loving god looking over them and protecting them. As of now we have not had that luxury. Until we do, it is necessary to continue judging god.

AFTERWORD

As we wrote this book, the authors realized that many good god-fearing people would believe that they have been insulted. We know that many fine people have been inculcated with religion and the concept of a supernatural being . For those people to give up a belief that their mothers and fathers taught them is difficult and for many of them it is impossible to do so.

However, we ask those good people to speak up when they see hatred and harm caused by religion – including their own religion. They may wish for heaven, they may even believe in life after death, but all must realize that life on earth is all that humans can control.

The authors have deliberately set out to criticize the JCM gods, but wish for good people to be happy with whatever god they choose to believe in, as long as no harm is caused to other people and to the environment.

RECOMMENDED READING FOR THE BRAIN – NOT THE HEART

Acharya, S. *The Christ Conspiracy*

Ali, Ayaan Hirsi *Infidel*

Barker, Dan *Losing Faith in Faith*

Blaker, Kimberly *The Fundamentals of Extremism*

Bloomer, Robert A. *Common Sense and the Bible*

Brogaard, Betty *Dare to Think for Yourself*

Campbell, Joseph *The Power of Myth*

Dawkins, Richard *The God Delusion*

Deitz, M. Lee *Questioning the Sacred*

Earl, Michael S. *Bible Stories Your Parents Never Taught You*

Garrod, Victor *The Demise of Christianity*

Harris, Sam *The End of Faith* and *Letter to a Christian Nation*

Harwood, William *Mythology's Last Gods*

Hayes, Judith *The Happy Heretic*

Henderson, John A. *God.com: A Deity for the New Millennium* and *Fear Faith Fact Fantasy*

Hitchens, Christopher *God is not Great: How Religion Poisons Everything*

Hoffer, Eric *The True Believer*

Ingersoll, Robert G. *On the Gods and Other Essays*

Kagin, Edwin F. *Baubles of Blasphemy*

Mattill, A.J. Jr. *Sweet Jesus*

Paine, Thomas *Age of Reason*

Russell, Bertrand *Why I Am Not a Christian*

Toynbee, Arnold J. *Civilization on Trial*

Turnbull, Charles *Trouble With God*

Willson, Harry *Freedom From God*

AND

Any *Holy Bible* by numerous authors

INDEX

ABOUT THE AUTHORS

John A. Henderson, MD graduated with honors from the University of Illinois College of Medicine in 1945. He interned at Research and Educational Hospital, Chicago, Illinois and completed his surgical training at Scott and White Clinic, Temple, Texas. He spent a career in the United States Air Force as a Flight Surgeon and General Surgeon. After retiring from the Air Force, Henderson practiced surgery in Asheville, North Carolina. He is now semi-retired and limits his medical activities to that of Medical Examiner for Buncombe County, North Carolina. Henderson can be reached at jrh828@webtv.net.

Craig Gurgew entered the United States Air Force in 1975 and served as an aircraft mechanic on jet fighter and transport aircraft. He graduated from Embry-Riddle Aeronautical University in 1979. Upon leaving the Air Force he became a commercial pilot and amassed over 14,000 hours in the air as a flight instructor and charter, corporate, and airline pilot. Gurgew resides in Hendersonville, North Carolina and builds homes as a licensed General Contractor and Real Estate Broker. Gurgew can be reached at craiggurgew@hotmail.com.

READERS' COMMENTS ON JUDGING GOD

At last, a physician willing and able to heal more than just bodies has combined with a builder who knows that a good foundation is critical – and that it has to be real instead of imaginary. Religious or atheist, no reader will ever be able to think about God the same way after reading this book. Dr. Henderson surgically removes any reasonable doubt about whether all of the "God" talk really makes any sense, while construction engineer Gurgew helps build a suitable coffin for the biggest lie of them all. The humor and plain language that Henderson and Gurgew bring to bear in this comprehensive case against the JCM gods (Henderson's shorthand for the Judeo-Christian-Muslim concepts of a personal God) may offend fearful religious people, but adults willing to look squarely at the truth will grow as they read. -- Ed Buckner, Southern Director, Council for Secular Humanism

Judging God is a simple, easy to understand book on the harmful effects of religion and the illogical beliefs of an all-powerful, all-knowing, supernatural being. It will not penetrate the inculcated brain of believers in a perfect God that makes no mistakes but it **will** appeal to all who care to think and consider the many gods of the world. -- William Harwood Ph.D., author of *Mythology's Lost Gods*

This book by Henderson and Gurgew is a bright beacon of light in a sea of darkness. What a wonderful inspiration and guide to those who are seeking the truth. The authors do not believe in life after death; however, they unwittingly have assured their own immortality through the inspirations of their writings. As long as a single copy of the book remains in print, it will live in the hearts and minds of the readers. This book should be prominently displayed in every library in America and be required reading in all Comparative Religion courses. -- Joseph Cunningham, Retired public school teacher, philosopher and biblical scholar

Judging God reveals the illogical beliefs of monotheism, a belief in an impossible God. In a day when people are "coming out of their closets" to claim that they are homosexual, agnostics, and atheists, this enlightening book should put the right-winged Christian-fundamentalist-bigots back into their closets of ignorance, irrationality, and illusions. -- Victor Garrod, Th.M., author of *The Demise of Christianity*

The beauty of this gem of a book is that it asks in plainspoken language the ethical and moral questions that both believers and nonbelievers should be addressing. Time after time, a case is made for why our lives would be enhanced in a religion-free world. The authors are proudly intolerant of the physical, scientific, and psychological religious abuses that are too often tolerated in a culture that promotes religious belief. -- Herb Silverman Ph.D., Secular Coalition for America, President

John Henderson and Craig Gurgew have penned a bold and biting critique of the world's most venerated sacred cow – God. In this age of rising sectarian violence, *Judging God* shines a desperately needed ray of moral clarity into a world blinded by religious faith. -- Michael S. Earl, author of *Bible Stories Your Parents Never Taught You*